THE BODY LANGUAGE ADVANTAGE

THE BODY LANGUAGE ADVANTAGE

Maximize Your Personal and Professional Relationships
with This Ultimate Photo Guide to Deciphering
What Others Are Secretly Saying, in Any Situation

LILLIAN GLASS, PH.D.
BEST-SELLING AUTHOR OF *TOXIC PEOPLE*

FAIR WINDS
PRESS
BEVERLY, MASSACHUSETTS

First published in the USA in 2012 by
Fair Winds Press, a member of
Quayside Publishing Group
100 Cummings Center
Suite 406-L
Beverly, MA 01915-6101
www.fairwindspress.com

16 15 14 13   2 3 4 5

ISBN: 978-1-59233-515-2
Digital edition published in 2012.
eISBN: 978-1-61058-407-4

Library of Congress Cataloging-in-Publication Data

Glass, Lillian.
The body language advantage : maximize your personal and professional relationships with this ultimate photo guide to deciphering what others are secretly saying, in any situation / Lillian Glass.
    p. cm.
ISBN 978-1-59233-515-2
1. Body language. 2. Nonverbal communication. I. Title.
BF637.N66G62 2012
153.6'9--dc23

                                        2012014774

Cover and book design by Traffic Design Consultants Ltd.
Book Layout by *tabula rasa* graphic design
Photography by Holly Randall and Chris Frawley

Printed and bound in China

Dedication

To my wonderful father, Anthony A. Glass, who, from my early age, taught me how to be an astute observer and pay close attention to people and everything else around me. I owe it all to you.

CONTENTS

PART II

INTRODUCTION

HOW WELL YOU READ OTHERS— AND WHY IT'S IMPORTANT THAT YOU DO

We live in the most amazing age when, in so many ways, life has become easy. Gone are the days of going to the library and searching for the books we need to give us the information we seek. We no longer have to wait in long lines to do our banking, pay our bills, buy a movie ticket, or pay for clothes we purchase. Now we can quickly do all these things and acquire anything we want from groceries to insurance and even find a relationship or a job just by pressing a few keys on a computer.

Things have become so easy and immediate that we don't even have to physically see or speak to anyone. Instead we can email, text, or instant-message them. But life does not exist on the Internet alone.

A great deal of life happens offline, where you must look at and listen to people face to face. Unfortunately, many of us are out of practice when it comes to face-to-face communication because of the technology today. If you don't know what others are really saying, you probably will misinterpret or even ignore the true message they are trying to communicate.

For instance, sometimes a person may say something that sounds harmless or benign, such as, "That's really great." But if the person makes this seemingly innocuous statement with an attacking burst of loudness on the word "great," he may mean something entirely different than you thought. His tone of voice could indicate sarcasm and mean the exact opposite.

If he exhibits a fistlike hand gesture, a stiff posture with a half-smile, and clenched jaw, you can bet he is angry. Now the comment "That's really great" takes on a different meaning.

But if you don't pay close attention to his vocal tone or body and facial language, you would perceive that all is well and nothing is wrong, when in fact there is something wrong and the speaker is obviously upset.

If you don't pay attention to communication patterns and body language, you will misread the message that people are trying to convey and place yourself at a huge disadvantage in your professional, interpersonal, and intimate relationships. Reading people appropriately allows you to direct the communication toward your advantage. It can make the difference between getting a job, closing a business deal, maintaining a friendship, and saving a marriage.

How to Recognize Conflicts and Cheating in a Relationship

The body doesn't lie and neither do voice or speech patterns. If you know how to read others, you truly have an added advantage over others. All relationships ebb and flow—if you can read what is really going on, you can help thwart potential problems.

For instance, you may hear your wife swallow her words at the end of a sentence so that they are inaudible as she tells you that everything is fine. But you will know that everything is not fine when you hear her monotone and observe her deadpan facial expression and leaning away from you as she speaks these words. Picking up on cues like these gives you the opportunity to open a dialogue about what is bothering her—perhaps you're spending too much time with your golfing buddies and not enough with her.

Reading body language and listening to vocal cues can help you figure out whether your spouse or lover is being faithful or whether the hottie you've been chatting up really likes you or is just being polite. Wouldn't it be great to know that there are certain body language "tells"—signals that involve the feet, hands, the way people lean or don't lean toward you—that let you know whether to keep talking or start walking?

Never Get Conned Again

Whether it is buying a car, venturing into a business deal, or dating someone who hasn't told you that he is married and has a house full of kids, one of the worst feelings is finding out that you have been conned, ripped off, or taken advantage of.

It's human nature to want to trust people. When they breach that trust it can be emotionally and financially devastating. Think back to a time when a particular person cheated you. In retrospect, were there any signals that may have told you something was amiss? Maybe he talked too much and too fast or went off on tangents. Maybe he stared at you without breaking eye contact. Maybe he was over the top in his compliments or too pushy and intimidating. Maybe his heel was off the ground and his toes were pointed toward the exit? Perhaps you noticed some of these signs but thought nothing of them at the time.

We have heard tragic stories about women who got involved with men married to several women simultaneously who were leading multiple lives. After these men are apprehended, the stories are similar: Victims report the red flags raised by the men's body language, facial expressions, what they said, and how they said it—but they either deliberately or subconsciously ignored these warnings. In the first chapter, I'll talk about the science behind listening to your instincts and how it can help you avoid situations like these.

Heading Off Work Disasters

How many people are shocked when they are fired or let go and never saw it coming? But looking back they see that there were body language signs that the boss or his assistant transmitted that indicated their time at the company was coming to an end. Maybe the assistant suddenly began to look down when talking to them or the boss started speaking in harsh staccato tones and furrowing his brow when addressing them. Perhaps if they had read these signals they would have been less surprised and better prepared for their inevitable exit.

Similarly, you could avoid getting your hopes up after a job interview and waiting for that never-to-come phone call if you had noticed that the interviewer barely looked at you, leaned back, took calls while you were there, and gave you a limp handshake and tight-lipped half-smile as she said, "Nice to meet you. We'll be in touch."

Having the Body Language Advantage is essential in our competitive environment where jobs are scarce and relationships are often fragile and fleeting. Knowing how to read others can make the essential difference in the quality of your life.

Knowing the Truth about the World around You

You can also gain a more accurate picture of what is going on in the news, from celebrities to politicians to sports figures, by having the Body Language Advantage. You will now be able to see whether these newsmakers are lying or telling the truth. You will be able to determine how they really feel about the people with whom they share relationships.

You will be able to see how certain political figures feel about one another and whether they mean what they say while they campaign for a particular office or are just reciting meaningless rhetoric. Are they merely reading lines written for them or speaking from their heart?

You will be able to quickly analyze whether someone involved in a scandal is telling the truth or spinning a tale. You may even be able to tell which sports team may win a game based on how well the players interact or don't interact with one another.

On another level, knowing how to read people can save your life and the lives of those you love. In an age when people commit desperate criminal acts and terrorism is on everyone's mind, it is essential to pay close attention to how people around you stand, walk, and talk. Doing so can provide you with clues as to whether you are in danger and allow you to make the decision to take appropriate action to ensure your safety and well-being. This book can help you do just that.

I have lectured to law enforcement officials across the country and in Canada on the body language of potential criminals, how to detect deception, and what to look for when a potential criminal may be ready to attack. Perhaps my biggest achievement and honor was being invited to speak at the FBI Academy in Quantico. Additionally, I have been called upon by detectives and private investigators to examine surveillance tapes and advise them whether the person may have had something to do with a particular crime.

Most of my work in applying my knowledge of body language has been with attorneys in criminal and civil cases. I have worked on cases in a variety of ways, including testifying as an expert witness in the area of behavioral analysis and vocal forensics in state and federal cases. I am able to assist attorneys by doing statement analyses of both the plaintiff and the defendant's depositions. My careful eye is often able to pick up information that may aid attorneys in their questioning as well as in the direction of their case.

From analyzing surveillance tape of a drug bust, for example, I was able to help determine the involvement of one of the key defendants. In criminal cases involving child molestation and sexual harassment, I was able to analyze the veracity of key witnesses and plaintiffs and show where on their deposition tape they may have possibly shown signs of deception or behaviors.

I am also very much attuned to the body language of terrorists, having studied countless videos of terrorists. I coauthored a book on the topic with former FBI special agent D. Vincent Sullivan, former manager of the FBI's Behavioral Analysis Program and a member of the FBI-Joint Terrorist Task Force. Together we put together an analysis for the public of what to look for when we may hear or see suspicious behavior.

Although *The Body Language Advantage* does not delve into the specifics of analyzing the body language of terrorists and criminal behavior, it does provide you with the basics of how to trust your guts when you suspect something does not seem right and what signals to look for in those who may deceive you so that you can avoid potential danger.

PART I

BODY LANGUAGE BASICS

CHAPTER 1

HOW TO DEVELOP YOUR AWARENESS: THE SCIENCE BEHIND TRUSTING YOUR INSTINCTS

IMPROVING YOUR AWARENESS of the world around you is crucial if you are to gain the Body Language Advantage. Doing so allows you to put the brakes on or stop yourself from entering potentially devastating situations or relationships, which can happen to even the most seasoned professional, highly educated individual, or street-savvy person.

HOW WELL DO YOU READ OTHERS?
Dr. Lillian Glass's Body Language Quiz

My quiz will provide you with the insight you need to determine how well you observe body language, facial patterns, and voice intonations. Answer each of the following twelve questions with the first thing that pops into your mind and determine your score at the end.

1. Every time I walk out of the house, I am completely aware of the people who are around me. TRUE / FALSE

2. The first thing I notice about a person is his or her face. TRUE / FALSE

3. I always notice what a person is wearing. TRUE / FALSE

4. If I don't like someone, I stop to analyze why that person rubs me the wrong way. TRUE / FALSE

5. I remember almost everything people say to me. TRUE / FALSE

6. I can usually tell whether someone is lying to me or stretching the truth. TRUE / FALSE

7. I usually remember how people stand, walk, or comport themselves in case I have to describe them to someone. TRUE / FALSE

8. If I had to describe the way someone spoke, I could easily recall it and describe it to others. TRUE / FALSE

9. When I am on vacation, I tend to notice the behaviors and actions of strangers, to which others seem oblivious. TRUE / FALSE

10. I remember how to get somewhere even though I may have been there only once or a few times. TRUE / FALSE

11. I can always tell what kind of mood someone is in. TRUE / FALSE

12. I listen carefully to people's tone, so I am aware of how they are feeling when they speak to me. TRUE / FALSE

Give yourself a point each time you answered "true" to a question and then add up your points.

If you answered "true" to all twelve questions, it means that you are very much tuned in to other people and your surroundings. You appear to be the kind of person who is on target in your assessment of others and someone who doesn't make many errors when you size someone up. You tend to be a lot more sensitive than others as you look more deeply at people and see who they really are instead of accepting them at face value. However, even though you received a perfect score, there is no doubt that you can fine-tune your already sensitive people-reading skills.

If you answered "true" to nine to eleven questions, it means that you have pretty good intuition most of the time. But there are times where you must feel like kicking yourself for not trusting your gut instincts. *The Body Language Advantage* can help you to become more decisive when it comes to assessing others.

If you scored six to eight, you probably don't like confrontation or altering the status quo. You tend to ignore the good and the bad in people, and you miss cues that others give off, which leaves you puzzled by what just

(continued on page 16)

happened. For instance, you may not realize that the person you have been chatting up isn't interested in you. You often wonder what you are doing wrong or believe that it must be Murphy's Law and just expect things to go wrong.

If you received a score of five or lower, you desperately need help and the information in this book! It appears that you walk around with blinders on. You may have a tendency to be so consumed with yourself and your own world that you lose sight of others. This lack of awareness of others makes you a prime candidate for getting ripped off, scammed by others, or hurt in relationships or business dealings. As you digest the information in this book, you may feel as though a veil has been lifted from your eyes as you begin to see and hear what others are really communicating a lot more clearly.

Now that you know how well you read people, let's get started by developing our awareness skills as we learn what to look for in people's body and facial language and their voice and speech patterns.

Did you ever think something just wasn't right but went ahead and did or said it anyway and later felt like a fool because you didn't listen to that little warning voice in your head? Whether it was getting involved in a bad relationship, job, or business venture, we do ourselves the biggest disservice by not listening to our instincts. Our body sends us an important message when our heart beats rapidly, we get an uncomfortable feeling in the pit of our stomach, we can't seem to catch our breath, we perspire, we feel tightness in our jaw or throat, or the hair on the back of our neck stands on end.

The message is: "Stop ignoring these body changes because your survival could depend on it." In this day and age, with high crime rates and terrorist threats, your safety may depend on tuning into your body's messaging system.

How Your Brain Helps You to Read People Better

Your brain consists of a right and left hemisphere covered by an outer layer called the cortex. There are four lobes, or areas, of the cortex, each of which have different functions. The frontal lobe deals with reasoning; the parietal lobe with sensory input; the occipital lobe with sight; and the temporal lobe, located on the left side of the brain, with speech, hearing, language, and memory. This crucial area houses Broca's area and Wenicke's area, major communication regions.

Below the cortex, deep within the brain, is the limbic system, which controls many of our emotions. It is in charge of our emotional responses to certain voices, tones, and speech patterns that we hear and behaviors and mannerisms that we observe. It also controls our "fight or flight" responses.

Our emotional responses vary from situation to situation. For instance, someone's high-pitched voice or specific comments may trigger an angry response from you, but they elicit a more positive or neutral response from someone else. The emotion or emotions we feel depend on what feelings we associate with particular body language, facial expressions, speech or voice patterns, and tones.

As we become more conscious of how the brain operates, we learn to access and stimulate the emotional centers of our brain much faster to help us detect certain danger signals. We need to integrate our cortex—where we objectively see, hear, speak, and remember information—with our limbic system, where we feel the wide range of emotions created by what we saw and heard. In other words, reading others depends on being in tune with your emotions, which are stimulated by what we hear in people's voices, speaking patterns, and the content of what they say as well as by what we see in their posture, body stance, movement, and facial expression.

Be wary of anyone who sets off negative alarms when it comes to these emotions. If, after listening to and observing a person, you begin to feel bad, never ignore that feeling. Then try to define the exact emotion you are feeling, such as anger, sadness, fear, boredom, or anxiety. Listen to your instincts and what they tell you. The only reason your initial instincts may be wrong is because you are not looking at or listening to what "is" but rather what you would like the person to be. You may be projecting positive traits onto that person that simply don't exist. It may be subconscious and wishful thinking on your part. Let's say you are introduced to a new coworker.

Reading others depends on being in tune with your emotions, which are stimulated by what we hear in people's voices, speaking patterns, and the content of what they say as well as by what we see in their posture, body stance, movement, and facial expressions.

You may overlook certain red flags because you may desperately want things to work out. The same applies to the new romantic interest in your life. You may overlook the obvious because you are determined to make that person into a potential mate. If you notice that someone is aloof and later discover she was merely shy, your instincts were right all along. There was something off about the person. She was indeed aloof and distant. After you've had a chance to get to know her, you know the root of the aloofness—she was shy and possibly intimidated by you.

Emotions Speak the Truth

Even if you try to hide them, your real emotions will eventually reveal themselves because the cranial nerves in the brain control both facial and vocal expression. So when you see a sudden and immediate facial or vocal change, that person's true feelings are being reflected. They are letting you know exactly what they think and how they feel about something.

To help you hone your people-reading skills, try one or more of the following exercises.

1. Stop, Look, and Listen

Remember when you learned to drive? You were taught to stop at a red stop sign, look for moving vehicles, and listen for any cars before you proceeded. If you didn't obey each of these rules, you could risk hitting a car or being hit by one.

Just as you shouldn't drive into traffic without looking and listening, you shouldn't run blindly into life. You have to stop and look at who is around you. You have to beware of body language and facial language. It is critical to open your eyes—and ears—to those around you.

Employ this same concept of stop, look, and listen the next time you meet a new person. As you shake his hand and ask him how he is, stop. Don't think about anything or anyone else. Focus on him. Now look at him. Observe his facial expression. Does he seem genuinely happy to meet you? Is he preoccupied? Does he have a dull, lifeless expression? Now listen to him. Listen to how he sounds when he speaks to you. Does he sound happy to meet you or bored? As he speaks, really look and listen to him. You will learn a lot. Try this with everyone you know. You will be amazed at what you learn about how a person really feels about you and others.

For instance, when Marla spoke to Jim and really stopped, looked, and listened, she observed that Jim shuffled his feet, moved around, and barely looked at her as they spoke. She also noticed that his tone was curt and wondered whether he was upset with her. Acting on her observations, she asked whether he was uncomfortable about something. He replied that he was thinking about calling someone at work about an important matter, which he had just remembered. Instead of concluding that Jim's body language and tone had something to do with her, she asked a question and discovered the real reason for his fidgety behavior.

2. The Emotional People-Watcher

This next exercise helps you to integrate what you perceive with what you feel about a person. The next time you have a few moments, start by relaxing your body. Take a small sip of air in through your mouth and then slowly release it. Whether you are seated or standing, consciously relax your head, neck, shoulders, arms, torso, legs, and feet—in that order. Observe a person sitting or walking in front of you, and as you do, think of an adjective that comes to mind that best describes that person, such as happy, ugly, cute, or strange.

Next, ask yourself whether the associated adjective was positive or negative and whether you felt good or bad toward that person. Even though the person is a stranger, there may be positive or negative feelings you will pick up from him or her based upon your observations. You should then ask yourself why the person elicited this particular emotional reaction from you. For instance, as Deborah did this exercise, she realized that whenever she saw someone with pursed lips she thought he or she looked mean and unfriendly. Mike began to notice that people who walked in wide strides appeared too forceful and bully-like to him, and that is why they tended to rub him the wrong way.

In essence, by doing this exercise you will begin to see patterns in people's body language and facial behaviors that do not sit well with you as you associate them with negative characteristics. Conversely, when you have a positive reaction to a stranger, you will become more aware of which body and facial language attributes appeal to you.

3. Improving Your Recall through Photos and Videos

Think of an event that happened about a year ago, when you were able to take photos or videotape it. Without looking at the photos or video, make a list of everything you remember about the event, such as whom you met, what you did, the color of people's outfits, the names of people, etc. If there was a meal, try and recall what you ate. Think of as much detail as you can remember. Now watch the video or look at the photos and see how many details you got correct and how your long-term memory fared. This exercise can help stimulate your memory and train you to become more aware of your surroundings.

Next, pull out other photos of people you know. Look at their expressions, how close they stand next to someone, and whether they lean in or away from that person. Pay close attention to what they are wearing and what they are doing with their hands and feet. Then analyze how they make you feel when you look at the photos. This exercise trains you to read between the lines and see what was really going on with the people in the photos at that particular time.

4. Movie-Watching with Sound Off and On

Next time you are on a plane and watching a film, don't use the headset. Just watch the film without sound. Try to figure out what is going on by carefully studying the actors' facial and body language.

When you arrive home from your flight, rent the movie and watch it with the sound turned on this time. See how much information you picked up or missed from watching the muted version. Repeating this exercise can help you pay close attention to facial expressions and body movements in others.

5. Fly on the Wall

The next time you are at a party where you don't know anyone or in a bar or restaurant on your own or waiting for someone, open your eyes and ears and concentrate on what the people near you are doing and saying. Listen to the tones of their voices and how they speak to one another. Are they kind to the person they are with or are they sarcastic and argumentative? How far do they sit from their companion? Do they touch them? Are they affectionate or do they ignore them? What does their body language say about them?

Observe couples interacting and guess by their body language and speech whether they are on a first date, have known each other for a while, are in love, or are headed for a breakup.

After doing these exercises on a regular basis, you will begin to see how much more astute you become in your analysis of other people.

CHAPTER 2

HOW TO READ BODY LANGUAGE BEHAVIOR

MANY PEOPLE erroneously think body language encompasses facial expressions and voice and speech patterns. In actuality, these are separate and equally important parts of the equation when it comes to reading people. You can, however, learn an enormous amount about what is going on in people's minds and even get a glimpse into their personalities by observing their body language alone. Body language involves the position, space, and movement of the body. The way people gesture, hold their posture, walk, stand, and move their arms and legs can give you a tremendous amount of information about them.

No matter how hard we try to suppress our emotions, a flash of genuine feeling will eventually escape, even if for a millisecond.

The body reacts in certain ways because it gets a message from deep within the brain to exhibit certain behaviors and movements that coincide with specific emotions that the brain has processed. For instance, let's say you see a physically attractive person across the room who smiles at you and says hello. Your eyes receive the message and transmit it to the upper portion of your brain (located in the back of the brain and called the occipital lobe) that there is a person across the room who has addressed you. Now your visual cortex (also located in the occipital lobe) processes that the person's face and body are in proportion. On further inspection, you notice that the person has dimples, thick, shiny hair, glowing skin, and a toned body. In addition, your ears pick up the sound that the person made, and then the upper left side of your brain processes what that person said and how she said it (i.e., the tone of her voice).

Deep within your brain, your limbic system kicks in, where you feel the emotions connected to what you just saw and heard. Your limbic system allows you to feel pleasant feelings about the person based on what you saw and heard. It translates the dimples, fresh-looking skin, toned body, and sultry voice. Your limbic system in turn stimulates the muscles in your face, body, and voice to react to what it perceives as positive, pleasant visual and auditory stimuli. You smile, move your feet in her direction, and brush your hair off your face to groom yourself before standing and walking over to introduce yourself.

Thus, there is an outer brain and inner brain connection that triggers a reaction to the people and things around you. This development was essential to our early survival. When, for example, the top layer of our brain acknowledged a salivating, open-jawed lion in front of us, the deeper part of our brain processed that this was not a good situation and we had better move our muscles so we could run to safety.

The same is true with people. Our limbic system processes how we feel about others, which sends the muscles in our body into action, reflecting how we react to them. No matter how hard we try to suppress our emotions, a flash of genuine feeling will eventually escape, even if for a millisecond.

The reason for this is because the body cannot lie. If you know the signals to look for, you will always be able to determine the truth about people's personalities and underlying motivations.

The Universal Language of the Body

Now that you understand the basics of how the brain influences your emotions, which affect your body and face movements, it is easier to comprehend that these processes are universal among people throughout the world. No matter what culture you are from, your body language is the vehicle that relays your emotions. When you are sad or feeling ashamed, your body retreats inward as your shoulders drop and your head bows down. When you are happy, your head is lifted, your shoulders are back, and your posture is erect. When you are afraid, your muscles tense, your eyes widen, and your jaw muscles contract tightly. When you are doubtful or uncertain, your head tends to be cocked to the side. When you are angry, your head lunges forward along with your lower jaw, your shoulders tighten, and the muscles throughout your body stiffen.

A person's body language can reinforce or contradict what they say. For example, a man may be discussing his wife and saying how much he loves her. But if he does so while shaking his head "no," covering his torso with one of his arms, shuffling his feet, or fidgeting with his hands, his body language is speaking more loudly than his words. He is telling us that something is wrong with his marriage.

The body has difficultly sustaining a lie because the brain directs the subtle body movements that reflect the truth. Now we are going to explore what specific body movements may mean, which can help you decipher what a person is really thinking or feeling.

What Leaning the Body Means

When you are fond of someone, there is a natural tendency for you to lean your body in the direction of that person.

In developing your people-watching skills, observe whether two people who know each other lean toward each other when they are sitting or walking together. If they lean their bodies toward each other, they share a mutual interest and attraction. Moreover, the angle of the lean and how physically close they are to each other may reflect the degree of intimacy in their relationship, which could be romantic or a close friendship.

If one person leans forward while the other leans back, it means that one is more interested than the other.

↑ If one person leans forward more than the other and this occurs while they are on a date or conducting business together, it suggests that one is not interested in or is turned off by the other.

✦ As you can see in the photo, this couple is very fond of each other because they are both leaning into the other.

If you observe both people leaning away from other another, they are definitely not into each other and there may even be some conflict in the relationship.

When Space and Territory Matter

A great deal of research has been done concerning how people react when their space and territory is infringed upon. This happens with animals that will stop at nothing to defend their territory, which often includes a mate. A male animal may kill another animal that infringes on his "female territory," just as some men will think nothing of fighting another man who may be interested in his girlfriend or wife. It is not just men who do this. Women do it as well.

Women may even turn their back on or give a cold shoulder to the other woman in an attempt to send the message that she is not welcome. This is typically an unintentional and automatic attempt to physically close off another person and keep her out of your space or territory.

When you see people standing right next to each other, it means they really like each other. But though this is often the case in Western cultures, it is not always true for societies in other parts of the world. In Latin and Middle Eastern cultures, people tend to stand and sit a lot closer to one another regardless of whether they like the person. It is important to keep these cultural considerations in mind when paying attention to a person's space and the distance they keep from others.

Standing close to another person can indicate intentions other than interest. For instance, when someone gets too close to you, it may be that he or she is trying to intimidate you. This closeness can often be seen as a hostile act. When people get too close for comfort, it is not uncommon to see expressions of annoyance or even aggression on a person's face when she feels her space is being invaded. Studies show that people react similarly when others get too close—they often retreat or withdraw as a means of trying to leave the uncomfortable situation. When people invade another's space, they may put that person on the defensive—for instance, prompting the person to become insecure about her hygiene, such as breath and body odor.

← When you see people standing far apart from one another, it usually means that they don't like or are threatened by each other. Research shows that those who stand at a far distance from others are often perceived as being arrogant or feeling superior. In many cases, however, distance can be used to gain the upper hand in an interaction. There is also the possibility that a person may be standing far away from you if he or she is feeling insecure, threatened, intimidated, or just plain does not like you!

⬆ If someone can't leave an uncomfortable situation, she may try several self-protective movements, such as using her arm to cover her torso or crossing both arms over her chest.

↑ You may pull back from the person opposite you and tuck your chin toward your chest as a means of self-protection during uncomfortable or awkward moments.

Mirroring is a technique often used by savvy salesmen who need to develop an immediate rapport with customers.

Tapping your foot or positioning your feet and legs to allow for a quick exit is a common sign of wanting to escape a situation. In addition, you may also assume a turtle-like position by raising your shoulders.

Mirroring: A Sign of Respect and Attraction

Let's say you are talking to someone and you place your hand on your chin, cock your head to the side, and place one of your legs is in front of the other. Suddenly you notice that the person with whom you are speaking does the exact same thing. This is a sign of mirroring behavior. In this case, it shows that your colleague is subconsciously taking your lead and looks up to and admires you.

Mirroring can also be done on purpose as a way to manipulate the other person. It was a common technique mentioned in many "how to find a mate" books back in the late 1970s and early 1980s. Women were told that to get a man to like them they needed to mirror his physical movements. If he scratched his head, then she was instructed to scratch her head. If he smiled, then she was supposed to smile. Although it may have been manipulative to get a man you liked to take notice of and relate to you, many women succeeded in getting to the next step with a man just by mirroring him.

Mirroring is a technique often used by savvy salesmen who need to develop an immediate rapport with customers. The more body language signals you have in common with clients, the more they can relate to you. The more they relate to you, the more they trust you, and the more they trust you, the greater the chances they will buy something from you.

⬆When people stand with their shoulders slouched and their head down, it usually means that they suffer from little or no self-confidence. Their posture may also indicate shame or embarrassment. No matter how well a person is dressed or how physically attractive, poor posture can negate anything positive about the image he or she wants to project to others. This stance indicates insecurity.

⬆If someone stands too rigidly or assumes a soldierlike posture, it signals that she may be uptight, inflexible, and perhaps a bit too precise and fastidious, to the point she can't relax. It is often very uncomfortable to be around people who stand or sit this way for long stretches of time because they don't put others at ease and seem to be constantly on guard.

⬆ A casual stance where there is flexibility and movement means that the person is at ease and comfortable with himself, which makes others want to be around him.

↑Certain stances can indicate aggression. When people turn to the side, not directly facing you, lift their head and cock it to the side, jut their chin, and stand with feet apart and hands in their pockets, they project hostility. Should one of their heels come off the ground, they may become verbally, even physically, abusive.

When people fidget, it is not uncommon to see them wringing their hands, rapidly moving their fingers, tapping on their arms, or even scratching themselves.

Rocking, Moving, and Fidgeting

When a person rocks back and forth or moves around a lot, it usually means that he or she feels anxious and uncomfortable and wants to get out of a situation or away from someone. The discomfort may also be because the person needs to go to the bathroom. And it is seen in those who are the bearers of bad news.

The rocking back and forth may also be a form of self-soothing and a means of physically calming themselves down. If you see someone doing this while speaking in front of a group of people, it often means that he feels nervous and uncomfortable and would prefer not to be standing in front of a crowd.

When people fidget, it is not uncommon to see them wringing their hands, rapidly moving their fingers, tapping on their arms, or even scratching themselves. It means they feel anxious about something. It may also be a sign of deception, that they are not telling the truth.

These kinds of movements may also indicate boredom. When people are bored, they often feel like falling asleep. So to keep themselves awake, alert, and energized, they often engage in extraneous hand movement. It may be a form of agitation, just as finger fiddling, tapping, and shaking may be signs that a person is angry, and the activity may be a way of subtly releasing their inner anger or anxiety.

→When people fiddle with their neck, tug at their collar, or even loosen their tie, they are literally getting "hot under the collar" or angry. Their emotions have caused their body temperature to rise and they are fidgeting to get immediate relief from the sudden surge of body heat.

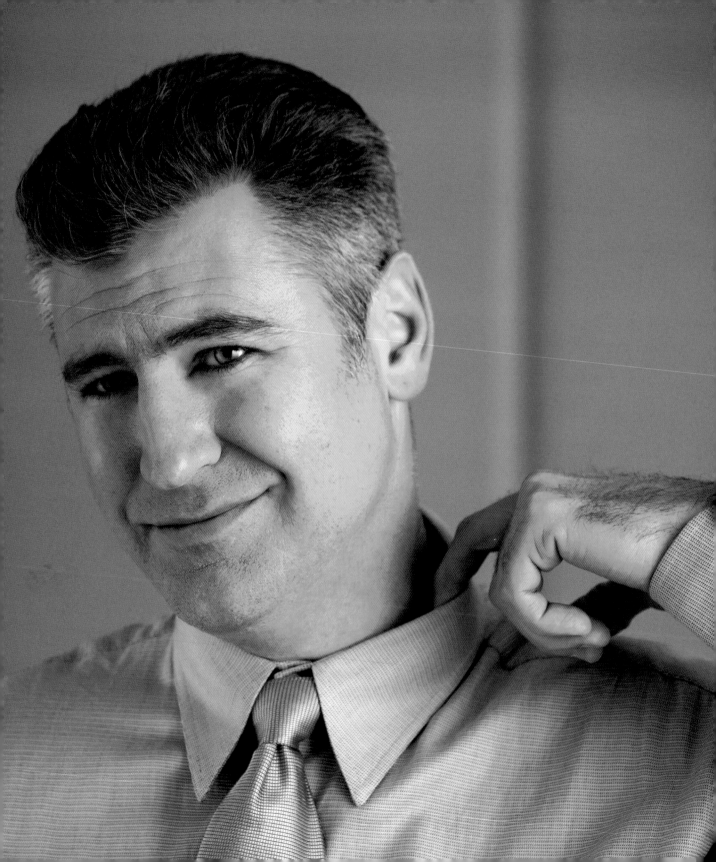

Head and Neck Positions

We can learn a great deal about what is really going on with people when we observe their head movements and the way they hold their head as they tilt, jerk, nod, bow, thrust, or scratch it. For example, tilting or cocking one's head to the side means different things depending on the circumstance. If someone tilts her head while listening to you, it can mean that she is either not processing or isn't sure of what you just said.

Most often, when someone tilts his head, you won't see a smile because the tilt means the person is unsure about something or someone. He may doubt something about himself or others. It may also be a signal that he is feeling insecure about something. In a woman, it may be interpreted as a sign that she is interested in someone as a head tilt is also considered flirtatious behavior.

When you see a person's head suddenly jerk backward, it means that she has literally been taken aback by something she heard or saw. She may tuck in her chin as she jerks her head back, which is usually a signal of surprise and shock. In criminal cases, it is not uncommon to see this body language behavior when someone is being interrogated and is asked a blunt question that hits too close to home.

In analyzing a police interrogation tape of a twenty-something-year-old man accused of armed robbery, I observed that he repeatedly denied all accusations as he sat calmly. Suddenly the interrogator threw out an unexpected question about where he had purchased his red baseball cap, a cap that a surveillance tape showed he had worn and lost during the robbery at the scene of the crime. The question took the suspect by surprise and his immediate response was to open his eyes wide and automatically jerk his head back. Although he denied that it was his cap, his body language gave it all away. Instead of being asked an easy question, such as whether the cap was his, he was asked where he bought it with the assumption that the cap was his. His head jerk told everyone that the cap was his.

When a person constantly nods his head, he subconsciously wants you to agree with him. He may be telling you a lie while nodding his head all along in hopes that you will agree with what he is saying.

← If a person is smiling while tilting her head, it may mean that she is being coquettish, especially if she tosses her hair and maintains eye contact with you.

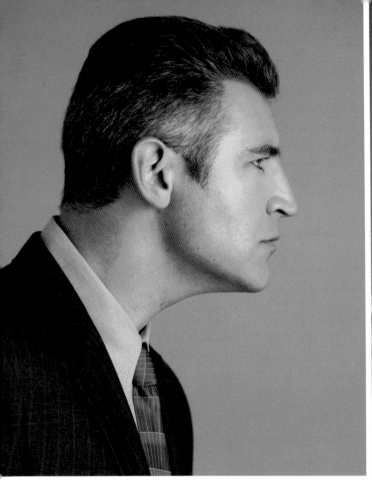 

⬆A forward thrust of the head means that the person is angry. He is the aggressor and most likely looking for a verbal or nonverbal fight. When someone thrusts and shakes his head at the same time, he is a step away from getting physically violent, so be aware.

⬆If someone touches and rubs the front of her neck immediately after hearing something, she may not only feel extreme anxiety, but vulnerable, too. The area around your throat and neck is the most vulnerable part of your body. It is involved in breathing and eating, so in essence, it is your lifeline. When a person grabs that area, she is instinctively protecting herself. You often see this throat-grabbing gesture when someone has just heard devastating news or has seen or experienced a sudden disaster.

A giveaway to people's true feelings is when they nod during a situation in which they should shake their head from side to side to indicate "no," and vice versa. For instance, a person may nod "yes" as she says, "I never cheated on you." In doing so, she has openly admitted that she did cheat. If she hadn't cheated, she would have been shaking her head from side to side, indicating "no."

In Western culture, when a person bows his head, it often indicates insecurity, subservience, and a lack of self-confidence. It may also signify embarrassment or guilt. If we recall the early photos of then-Lady Diana before she married Prince Charles, we clearly see a self-conscious, insecure, and demure Diana who always appeared to have her head bowed. It was not until she began to feel more confident in her role as Princess Diana and received public adulation from around the world that she began to hold her chin and head high.

Scratching your head can be a self-soothing gesture to indicate that you are thinking. If you are feeling particularly tense, scratching your head may be a way to calm yourself down and deliver some immediate, feel-good physical gratification. Remember how great your scalp feels when your hair gets washed at a salon? Scratching your own scalp gives you a similar feel-good sensation, especially if you are feeling tense, anxious, or perplexed.

When people are thinking about something, feel confused, or are not sure what to do, they often become tense. That tension can affect the muscles in their head and scalp. There can also be blood-flow changes in the head and scalp area that create an itching sensation. Head scratching is a way of relieving that tension and self-soothing.

It can also indicate that a person is not telling the truth. When people lie, their autonomic nervous system takes over. That means their blood flow changes and capillaries enlarge to accommodate the increased blood flow. This often causes an itching sensation.

If after hearing something, someone suddenly touches the back of her neck and begins rubbing it, she is usually feeling extreme anxiety about what she just heard.

The Story of the Shoulders

You can tell a great deal about people by the way they hold their shoulders. For example, if their shoulders are ramrod straight and pulled back in a military-like posture, it may indicate that they are rigid, uptight, or have a nonflexible type of personality. A person who holds this shoulder position usually keeps his arms close to his sides, with elbows tucked in. Whether sitting or standing, the legs tend to be close together, and the walk is somewhat mechanical, which matches the shoulder position.

✦ Whenever I am asked to analyze a celebrity couple's photo for a magazine to determine the state of their relationship, one of the first things I look at is how they position their shoulders in relation to each other. When I see one person in the photo with one shoulder raised higher than the other, I know that the relationship may be in trouble. In essence, one person is getting the "cold shoulder" or being frozen out of the relationship, and the other person's shoulder is serving as a barrier between the two.

✦ Slumped and rounded shoulders often indicate that a person lacks confidence. Slumped shoulders are often associated with insecurity and a lack of self-esteem. They may also be indicators of depression or sadness. This posture literally says that the person is "shouldering a burden" or feels a heaviness as though he has the "world on his shoulders."

By contrast, if a person's shoulders are straight yet relaxed, it indicates that he possesses a great deal of self-confidence. This confident type of posture is often accompanied by an open body position with both the arms and legs uncrossed when sitting or standing. When speaking, they freely use their hands to express points.

People who display rounded shoulders tend to be those who retreat or withdraw from a situation, unlike their straight-shouldered counterparts. This can be valuable information when you are involved in a business negotiation. For instance, in a business negotiation, if you see someone's shoulders suddenly hunch over, chances are they are not feeling very secure about what they are offering in the negotiation process—it may reveal that there is some wiggle room to negotiate further.

When you see people shrug their shoulders, it may be a sign of embarrassment, insecurity, or deception. The latter depends on the subject and context of the communication. For instance, if you think that your mate is cheating and you ask her whether she is having an affair, a shoulder shrug may indicate she is embarrassed that she just got busted as she literally attempts to "shrug it off" and not make a big deal about it.

When you see a person with both of her shoulders pulled up, it means that she is feeling defensive. It shows that she is closing herself off to you or to the situation. It may be because she is embarrassed, uncomfortable, intimidated by you, or simply doesn't like you. She is creating a protective physical barrier with her shoulders so that she may hide from you because she is feeling vulnerable and insecure.

You often see children raise their shoulders when they feel guilty about doing something they should not have been doing.

Whenever you see a person with both of his shoulders lunged forward, it is a signal of aggression. Typically, his arms are crossed and his fingers are exposed, touching or grabbing on to his biceps. He is letting you know that he is ready for a fight and ready to take you on verbally, physically, or both.

← **When people with a chip on their shoulder angle their shoulders to the side, there is a greater chance for a physical altercation.**

What Our Hand Language Reveals

You can often tell a person's emotional state by the position of her hands—whether she is open and happy, closed off and sad, secure, independent, emotionally expressive, reserved, worried, insecure, anxious, bored, or mad.

I am frequently asked if it is a good or a bad thing when people use their hands when they speak. I say that is a good thing unless they go overboard. In certain cultures, using a lot of hand and arm movement when speaking is the norm, while in other cultures people tend to be less inclined to use hand movements. Generally, using your arms and hands when you speak gives added emphasis to what you are trying to communicate. When people move their arms away from their body as they gesture, it indicates that they tend to be more open and less reserved.

If you see strong, flowing hand movements when a person is speaking, it indicates that she feels self-confident about what she is trying to communicate. When people are emphatic about their beliefs and emotional about what they are saying, you will usually see this reflected in the amount and degree of arm and hand movement they use.

There are times when the person speaking to you will do so with both hands clasped behind him. This indicates the ultimate in self-confidence. He is exposing his entire torso, which indicates that he has nothing to hide and he feels secure and open. This stance is not uncommon with law enforcement officers.

If someone places her steepled hands in front of her mouth, it usually means she is confident or sure about her judgment and what she is about to say. It is a gesture that also tends to indicate that she is being truthful.

A person's confidence will also be reflected in his handshake. If he touches the palm of your entire hand with his and firmly presses his palm against yours, he is feeling good about himself and confident about being in your presence. He is displaying openness and a sense of security.

Anything other than this type of handshake shows a lack of confidence or an indication that the person isn't receptive to you. If someone gives you only her fingers to shake or she barely touches you or gives you a quick touch of a handshake as though she can't wait to get away from you, it screams low self-confidence, fear, or a sense of intimidation on her part.

✦When a person is being open and honest, you will notice that the palms of his hands are exposed and his fingers are extended as he speaks. When a person shows his palms, he is making himself vulnerable to the person he's speaking with. This gesture shows that he has nothing to hide.

✦When people hold their fingers open and their hands parallel to each other, it shows self-confidence.

⬆ When a person feels insecure, he will often curl his fingers and not extend them, thereby minimizing the size of his hands. This can also occur when a person is being deceptive or is angry.

⬆ When a person is feeling insecure or full of anxiety, it is not uncommon to see her pick at her fingers or hands. It can be a signal of deception when it is done suddenly in response to a significant question.

✦ When a person is confident, you may see him touch each fingertip of one hand to the other hand to form a steeple-like position. This gesture is usually made in front of the body when a person is actively listening and confirms that he is being attentive, open, and receptive to what you have to say.

Insecure Arms and Hands

A person who constantly touches you when he speaks displays insecurity as he seems unable to communicate unless he has your full and undivided attention. It often shows a lack of boundaries as well. Though it is considered annoying and offensive in Western culture, excessive touching when speaking to another person is the norm in other societies.

Usually when people tell you the truth, they show you the palms of their hands. Also, when a person is lying, you may see him suddenly cross his arms over his torso. This indicates that he is physically closing himself off to you.

Hand fidgeting or moving the fingers around when they are interlocked or facing the fingers of the other hand often indicates deception.

Also, people may deceive you by hiding their hands. They might roll them into a ball, thereby hiding their fingers. They may sit on their hands or put them fully in their pockets so you can't see them. This is in contrast to people who have part of their hand or thumbs exposed in their pockets. If their hands are in their pockets and the thumbs are up, it shows confidence. If their thumbs are down, it shows insecurity.

If a person is not telling you the truth, she doesn't have to hide or show excessive movement with her arms or hands. Instead, she may simply hold a pose and never deviate from that position. She may hold on to her elbows or clasp her hands together without moving them. You often see muscle tension or pressure in the hands as they hold on tightly to themselves.

You may even see people holding on to a table or the sides of a chair to ground themselves as they spin their web of deception. The important thing to notice is that they do not move at all, and their unyielding rigidity is what gives them away.

If someone is feeling uncertain, she will have a tentative grip as she touches you. If it happens in your personal life, it means that the person isn't sure how you will respond to her touching you or she is insecure, uncomfortable, or intimidated by you.

← **When you see someone with a pleading hand gesture in which she shows you the backs, not the palms, of her hands, chances are she is not telling you the truth and is hiding something.**

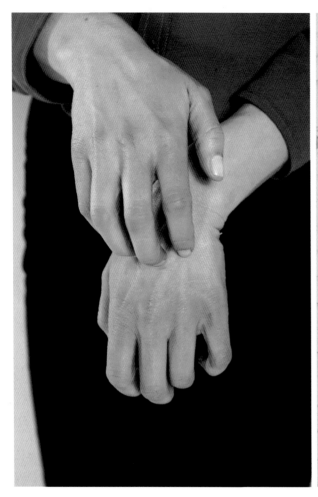

↑When people suddenly scratch their hands—either their palms or the back of their hands—there is a good chance that they are lying to you. This is because of the blood-flow changes that occur when a person lies; the capillaries expand, which often creates an itching sensation.

↑It is not uncommon to see people hide their hands when they lie to you.

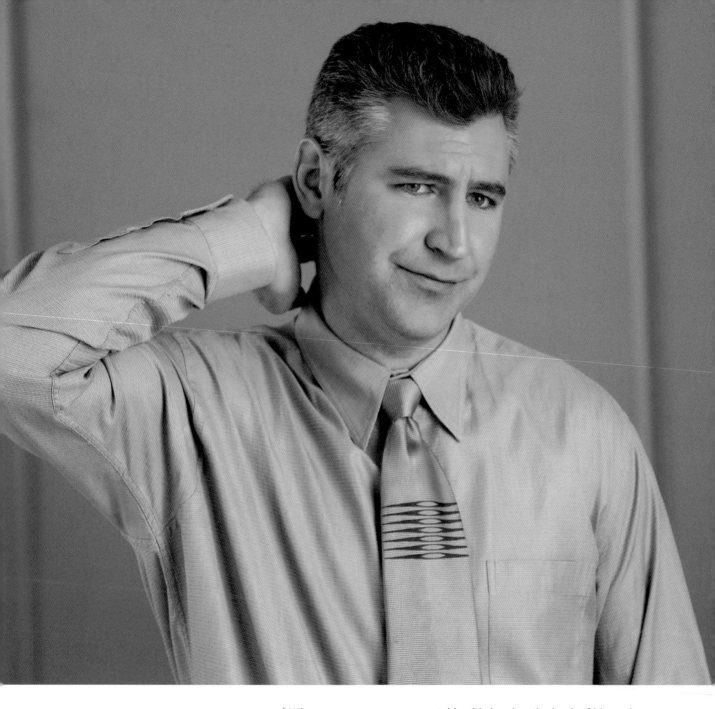

↟ When you see someone scratching his head or the back of his neck, it often means that he is feeling uncertain about something. Pay attention to the person's face, which may exhibit a quizzical or confused expression.

↑If someone gives you the "dead fish" handshake, it means that she is bored by you, doesn't like you, or is feeling socially inept or insecure around you.

↑A person will move his hands a great deal when feeling anxious, and he may not to stop until the anxiety is allayed. The muscles in his hands and arms will tense up. Often, you will see him continuously rubbing one hand over the other as though he is wringing out wet clothing. This behavior is a form of self-soothing that has a calming effect.

↑ You may see a person who is anxious and worried cross her arms and rub each arm with the opposite hand. During times of stress and angst, the body temperature often drops, creating a sensation of coolness. This subconscious arm rubbing functions to warm the body during stressful periods, and it is also a form of self-soothing.

No matter what culture you are from, when someone points a finger at you, it is a hostile gesture. The closer your index finger gets to the person, the greater the degree of anger.

When a person is bored, he will make a number of varied hand movements. It is a subconscious way of creating activity in an attempt to keep himself occupied. You will see him literally twiddling his thumbs and systematically roll one thumb over the other as he clasps his hands together. Abrupt changes in hand movements are also indicative of boredom. You may also see large, flailing arm movements, which suggest restlessness.

A handshake gives you clues about someone. If a person is worried or anxious, she may use a handshake that either feels stronger or is held longer than usual.

Self-mutilating behaviors such as finger biting, finger pulling, nail biting, and cuticle picking indicate anxiety. Sometimes creating physical pain redirects or helps assuage the emotional pain caused by anxiety.

In photos of celebrity "frenemies," you'll often see people smiling with clenched fists. It may seem as though the two people like each other and may even go so far as to hug. But the truth is revealed in their fists. It shows that there is anger and disdain underneath their phony smiles and superficial gestures of friendship. If you are on the lookout for this gesture when you are around people you know socially or do business with, you will quickly discern who is friend and who is foe.

No matter what culture you are from, when someone points a finger at you, it is a hostile gesture. The closer your index finger gets to the person, the greater the degree of anger, and the greater the likelihood of a physical altercation.

← Even if a person's facial expression doesn't look angry, when you see someone with a clenched fist, rest assured that she has hidden anger inside.

A person can display anger through thumb gestures. For instance, someone who sticks to her position in the middle of a discussion may hold her hands in a fist, with her thumbs stiffly positioned upward. It means that the person is firmly planted in her position and will fight till the end for what she believes.

People's handshakes may also reflect their level of hostility. If they give you a hard, crushing handshake, it may not only reflect their anger toward you, but also their competitiveness with you. Using a handshake at the outset to show you how strong they are is a ploy to intimidate you.

It's also possible that a person who is either angry with you or doesn't like you may refuse to shake your hand and will merely nod or give you a fleeting handshake while barely looking at you.

The Language of the Legs and Feet

If you want to know how a person really feels about you or whether he is lying, look at his legs and feet. Though it may be possible to temporarily manipulate one's facial, arm, and hand gestures, it is essentially impossible to control one's foot and leg movements. The brain sends out a signal via the limbic system—the emotion command center—which triggers the muscles, including the larger, more cumbersome, and more difficult to manipulate muscles in the legs and feet. That is why the lower extremities give away more information about how a person honestly feels in a given situation.

The way a person stands and sits and walks can also give you reliable clues about the type of person with whom you are dealing. For example, the expression "their feet were firmly planted on the ground" says it all when it comes to dealing with a person who is honest and forthright. A person who is solid and open stands with both feet evenly spaced apart, a position that suggests he has nothing to hide.

If a person sincerely likes you, you will notice her toes pointed in your direction, whether she is sitting or standing. The closeness of her feelings toward you is often reflected in how close her toes are to yours.

How a person walks can also signal hostility. If they take large steps and make loud, clumping noises with their shoes, they are probably harboring inner anger.

✦ If someone speaks to you with a hand on the hip, it is a sign of arrogance. If they have their arms akimbo, it means they are angry. It is also an aggressive gesture that carries hostility and says, "Keep your distance."

↑When sitting, if the legs are crossed at the knee, it shows confidence, openness, and self-assuredness.

⬆ When a man in particular sits with his leg resting on his knee, he is showing overconfidence that verges on arrogance.

When people walk at a steady pace with a slight bounce in their step, it shows self-confidence and a sense of happiness. The arms swing at their sides, and they often have a relaxed and contented look as they walk.

↑People who are depressed or sad tend to have a delicate, often tip-toe-like walk. They take small steps, rounding their shoulders and holding their head down toward their chest as though they are preoccupied with thought. They usually walk at a slower pace than others.

When people lie, it is almost impossible for them to keep their feet from moving or shuffling.

Insecure Legs and Feet

People who feel timid or insecure tend to hide their feet when they sit. They will often pull their legs together and lean them over to the side so as to not take up much space.

People will engage in foot jiggling and foot tapping to indicate their impatience and desire to leave.

If you are standing next to a person whose toes are not positioned in your direction, it means that he is not interested in you socially or professionally.

People who take up a lot of room by stretching out their legs display dominance and disrespect toward you, as well as inner hostility. It is their attempt to be noticed and let you know that they are in charge; one often sees this behavior with bullies. Foot shuffling and leg kicking and swinging are also signals of inner hostility.

Oftentimes, people who are lying keep their body stiff as a board. They will hold on to themselves as a support for their rigid body so that they don't give away the fact that they are lying to you. You may ask them a direct question, such as, "Were you drinking at the bar last night?" They may stare directly at you without blinking an eye or moving a muscle in their face. They may clasp their hands together with their elbows firmly planted at their sides as they calmly reply, "No, I wasn't there." As calm, cool, and collected as they are in their upper body, the complete opposite is going on below the waist. When people lie, it is almost impossible for them to keep their feet from moving or shuffling.

→ **When a person wraps her foot around her leg or locks her ankles by placing one foot over the other, she is letting you know that she is not feeling secure or self-confident.**

⬆If you are at a business or social event with someone and notice that his heel is off the ground when sitting or even standing, it is not a good sign. It means that he wants to get away from you.

⬆If a person doesn't want to be with you or holds back from communicating with you, it is not uncommon for you to see her feet crossed at the ankles, and she will remain in that stationary position throughout your interaction. It indicates that she isn't going to budge or reveal anything of significance about herself, essentially closing herself off to you.

The Body Language Grooming and Clothing

Thus far, we have seen how the way your body moves can speak volumes about you. But so does the way you dress and groom yourself. Although a discussion on the body language of grooming and fashion could easily merit its own book, for the purpose of this section I will address essential issues that are particularly revealing.

For instance, people who do not pay attention to hygiene—such as having a clean body, washed hair, brushed teeth, fresh breath, clean hands, and clean clothes—may have self-esteem issues. They may also be suffering from depression, in which case their last concern is how they look, let alone how they look to others. For them, it is hard enough to get out of bed. If, however, you have known a person to be well groomed and then see a sudden and dramatic change in their appearance or hygiene, he may be going through a rough patch, such as the loss of a job, a divorce, or health problems.

If a middle-aged woman wears her hair long, past her waist, it may indicate an attempt to hang on to her youth. It may also reflect a sense of insecurity and low self-esteem. One often sees overly long hairstyles in women older than forty in Hollywood, where youth is a critical factor in the entertainment industry.

Men are not immune to hanging on to their youth as reflected in their use of hair transplants, toupees, and hairpieces. Men who purchase hair plugs or toupees can suffer from low self-esteem and insecurity because they are hiding who they really are. This applies to women as well who constantly change their hairstyle and color.

With makeup and the advent of surgical enhancements and cosmetic treatments that promise younger appearances, more people are eager to improve their looks as they age. But when you observe that they have gone overboard with surgery after surgery and overinflated lips and cheeks that make them look cartoonish, it screams volumes about their psyche. It shows how unsatisfied they with themselves deep down. It betrays a level of hopeless insecurity and feelings of not being worthy or up to par, which often spills over into their personal and business interactions with others.

CHAPTER 3

HOW TO READ FACIAL LANGUAGE

FACIAL MOVEMENTS AND EXPRESSIONS are how people position their face when listening or speaking. Throughout the centuries, faces have told us a great deal, as depicted in the works of Rembrandt to modern-day photojournalism, and many of these facial expressions have been etched in our minds forever.

When someone's facial expression does not match his words, there is trouble.

Facial language can provide us with insight into a person's frame of mind and mood. For instance, when people are sincere, their face is open and their expression corresponds to what they say. Their gaze is soft and welcoming, and their face is relaxed, lacking in tension.

When someone's facial expression does not match his words, however, there is trouble. When someone says he loves you but his facial expression is devoid of emotion, chances are he doesn't really love you. Instead, his true feelings are clearly displayed on his face for you to see.

Forehead Forecasting

People's foreheads give us a lot of information about them. But reading the facial language of the forehead can be more complicated these days with the advent of wrinkle fillers and the chemical Botox, which essentially paralyzes the facial muscles in an attempt to make people appear younger.

When you see forehead lines or wrinkles that are positioned horizontally and raised upward, it means that the person is surprised. You will also see these upward lines on someone who likes you when she first sees and greets you. These lines are often accompanied by raised eyebrows and eyes that are wide open. In essence, their facial language is saying that they are pleasantly surprised to see you.

A raised forehead can indicate surprise when a person is caught lying or doing something he shouldn't. For instance, you'd be wise to look at the forehead of someone being interviewed about a crime in which he may have been involved.

When a person blushes, usually the first area to show the red pigment is the forehead, which may also indicate that the person is sexually or emotionally aroused, excited, or agitated.

When people experience sudden tension, you will often see them rubbing their forehead either to remove sweat or moisture or to soothe themselves. You commonly see this facial gesture when

A wrinkled forehead can also indicate someone's displeasure at seeing you. That expression is similar to when a person is in pain, worried, or concerned about something. These wrinkles can appear as vertical lines in the middle of the forehead, above the nasal bridge.

When a person is lying or distressed, the forehead tends to show moisture or sweat before any other place in the body. A sudden shine will appear on the forehead as the autonomic nervous system kicks in and the body releases stress in a physical way.

The eyes often tell how a person feels about us.

people feel confused. Then, when their confusion clears and they figure out what to do or realize they made a mistake, you will often see their open palm slapping the middle of their forehead. Rubbing the forehead at the temples also helps relieve stress.

Another indicator of stress or tension is when you see veins popping out of a person's forehead. You see this happen to celebrities on the red carpet where they are under a lot of stress as countless cameras flash at them. Depending on the context in which you ask someone a question, pulsating temples can mean either stress and anxiety or deception.

The Eyes Have It

The eyes provide a tremendous amount of information, such as whether a person is telling the truth or what emotions she is most likely experiencing. In addition, the eyes often tell how a person feels about us.

When a person likes you and first sees or meets you again, his eyes become wide and circular as though he wants to take in your presence visually. Someone who is attracted to you will "cross gaze," in which he looks to the left, sweeps his eyes across your face, and then looks to the right, repeating this behavior without settling his gaze upon you directly. As he processes his attraction to you, his eyebrows will barely raise. However, as he mirrors your facial expressions, his eyes and brows will do what your eyes do. Someone who likes or loves you can't keep his eyes off of you. He will always look at you when he speaks and he will notice even the most minute things about you. He may also verbally describe your actions and reactions to you: for instance, "Look at how your dimples come out when you smile," or "You looked embarrassed and turned away when I said that."

When someone is in love with you, he tends to look at you with a soft gaze and his eyes may appear to glisten. This is the autonomic nervous system at work as it secretes lubrication throughout the body, including the eyes.

↑If someone really likes you, she tends to look at you for longer periods than she would otherwise. Moreover, her pupils may enlarge as she looks at you steadily, without breaking her gaze.

↑ When someone is surprised or astonished, her eyes will open wide, and you'll see the sclera, which is the whites of her eyes, above the iris, which is the colored part of her eyes. Anticipating this surprise response will help you easily spot it after confronting a person in a lie. The expression of surprise often accompanies a raised eyebrow and forehead and a slack jaw or open mouth.

↑ A person who is afraid will also have a wide-eyed appearance, but the main difference is that all of the sclera tends to be visible. The jaw, instead of dropping in surprise, will tense and usually pull back in a horizontal position.

When the Eyes Give Away a Lie

When people have something to hide, they have a hard time looking at you. Even if someone smiles at you, spreads her lips horizontally, and shows some teeth, if her eyes don't squint or crinkle when she smiles, the happy feelings that she is attempting to display are false. There are many things the eyes do that signify extreme stress and or deception, such as:

- Rapid blinking or fluttering when listening to or speaking about critical issues
- Shutting when a crucial question is brought up or discussed
- Constant staring without breaking eye contact
- Sudden, uncontrollable muscle twitching, which signifies that the autonomic nervous system is activating the muscle movement

↑Someone is angry at you when he doesn't smile, has a tense facial expression, and stares at you without breaking his gaze. It also means that his aim is to intimidate, dominate, or threaten you. The forehead also may have a vertical line or wrinkle of distress in the middle.

↑When someone doubts or disbelieves what you are saying, he will narrow his eyes, furrow his eyebrows, wrinkle his forehead vertically, and slightly squint one eye. Usually there is an accompanying lip movement in which one of the sides of the lips is pulled back tightly. The lip pull, which means someone is feeling discomfort or thinking about how to manufacture a story, is usually in sync with the same eye that is squinted.

• Suddenly opening wide when crucial information is presented
• Suddenly shifting the gaze to the left or to the right, up or down, or looking around

Although one school of thought believes that when you look in a certain direction it means something, there is no scientific evidence to prove this. What is known is that when a person suddenly shifts her gaze, she is showing discomfort or thinking about how to manufacture a story.

When a person is angry, you will often see the sclera underneath the iris as opposed to seeing it above the iris, which happens when someone is surprised or afraid. Often a furrowed eyebrow and vertical wrinkle in the forehead will accompany this angry eye expression. The eyes may narrow as both the upper and lower eyelids tense up, especially during a confrontation with another person. This muscle tension may be nature's way of protecting the eyes before a potential physical fight.

People look down when they lie, are embarrassed they lied, got caught in their lie, or feel so guilty about something they can't look at you. By looking down and averting their gaze, they avoid your judging them with a look of anger, disappointment, or disgust.

If you know what to look for, you can tell when a smile is genuine or forced.

Reading Lips

Paying close attention to people's lips can teach you how they feel about you and others and whether they are being truthful. If you practice regularly, you may become an actual lip reader and learn to read lips just based on people's oral movements around their lips, tongue, and teeth.

Just as forehead sweating is a visible sign of tension and possible deception, so is above-the-lip perspiration. This area and the forehead are the first places perspiration accumulates as the autonomic nervous system begins to throttle into high gear in response to sudden changes in the body. As the temperature rises in the body, it starts to perspire. So when you see upper-lip sweat, deception may be a huge possibility, especially when the temperature in the room does not merit sweating and when you didn't notice that the person's upper-lip was sweating earlier.

When it comes to smiling, some people feel obligated to smile even when they don't want to because they feel it is the right thing to do to seem polite. But if you know what to look for, you can tell when a smile is genuine or forced.

Celebrities tend to display tight-lipped smiles when the paparazzi are shooting their photos. They may not be happy about the invasion of their space, but they try to be polite, and they don't want a bad photo taken of them or to alienate their fans. They will tighten their lips and pull them horizontally to give the impression they are smiling, but deep down they are not feeling it.

Even if you see someone's teeth, a smile can still be phony if you don't see the person's eyes smiling as well.

A phony, tense smile may occur when someone is grieving or in a bad situation. This is confusing and upsetting to those who are also in mourning or upset about the same situation as the person who is smiling nervously. For example, when former president Jimmy Carter spoke about the Iranian hostage crisis during his time in office, he usually had a tight-lipped smile, which was disconcerting to the public because it was so at odds with the gravity of the situation. Should you see someone display a tight-lipped smile in the face of a tragedy, he is probably as nervous and uneasy as you are but expresses it differently.

✦People who are shy, embarrassed, or ashamed will have a hard time looking at you and maintaining eye contact because of their low self-esteem and discomfort with any attention given to them. You will often see them looking down or gazing around the room.

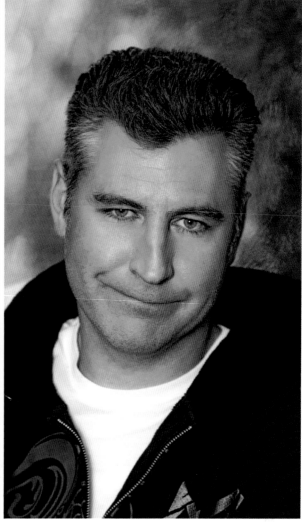

When someone really likes you, it shows in her smile. With a heartfelt smile, as we learned earlier, the eyes crinkle, especially around the outside corners. The corners of the lips turn upward, and the lips part, showing the teeth. The apples of the cheeks are raised and resemble puffy balls. A person whose smile is genuine radiates happiness, prompting those around her to smile in return because her smile is open and indicates safety and comfort.

If you see someone smiling at you but his eyes are not crinkling, his cheeks are not raised, or he doesn't show his teeth, the smile is fake.

✦When people show their teeth in a fake smile, the teeth and jaws are clenched together, unlike a real smile where more of the teeth are showing and the jaw is open. You often see this type of grin in photos of little kids who are forced by their parents to smile for pictures.

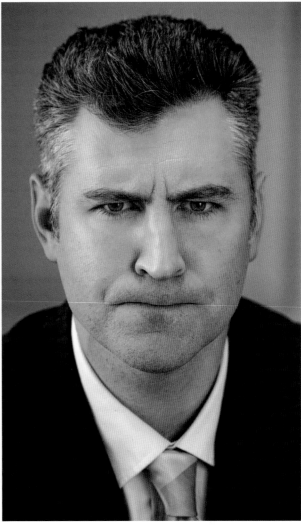

⭷People under stress will display a tense, tight-lipped smile. It is their subconscious way of trying to make things more pleasant by trying to eliminate and mask their tension. But they do not succeed because the tension is evident in their lips and jaw.

⭷A tight-lipped, frowning expression means that a person is angry and that nothing can get the information out of him. He is not only holding back information but also trying to stifle his emotions.

Be on the lookout for a genuine smile at an inappropriate moment. For instance, someone who smiles during a discussion of your boyfriend's infidelity is probably and secretly thrilled that you two are no longer a couple.

You also see genuine smiles known as "duping delights." When someone lies to you and thinks she got away with it, if you confront her, you will usually get a verbal denial but see a genuine smile and even hear a chuckle. This is more often than not a signal of guilt on their part.

Smiles occasionally indicate the withholding of information. When people purse their lips into a slight smile, it means that they know something but they are not going to tell you. You see it with celebrities who may be asked about a romance they don't wish to reveal publicly. Their smile indicates ambivalence: They are happy about the relationship but unhappy and unwilling to discuss it.

Lip biting is a subconscious way of holding yourself from speaking. It is a typical reaction that the facial muscles make when a lie has been told. The lower lip recoils while the upper teeth clamp down on it.

In the case of lip blowing, the person is filled with the tension that builds before or after making an attempt at deception. As the autonomic nervous system works overtime—blood pumping, heart beating—respiratory changes take place in the body to maintain a homeostatic balance. Thus people will often take in a huge breath of air through their nose or mouth and forcibly and audibly blow it out through their lips.

Lying Lips

When people lie, it is not uncommon to see them place a hand over their mouth, which indicates they literally don't want to speak the truth. They are in essence making a hand signal over their mouth in a subconscious attempt to shut themselves up.

In addition to lip licking due to the dryness of the oral mucosa, which creates "cotton mouth," watch for someone's throat muscles to tighten and an up-and-down bobbing motion of the neck or Adam's apple as he literally tries to swallow his lie.

← When someone is speaking but trying to manufacture a story, it is not uncommon to see the "lip swing," in which she pulls her lip to one side of her face as she ponders what lie to make up next. You may also see this expression when people are confused or trying to determine what to do next.

⬆ Lip biting, fiddling, and blowing are other indications that people may be lying, especially when crucial information is presented to them.

⬈ Lip licking can be a signal of deception. When people are under stress or lying, the saliva in their mouth tends to dry up, giving them "cotton mouth." This causes the inside of their lips or mucosa to feel dry and uncomfortable and their teeth to stick to the inside of their lips. You will then see them lick their lips or teeth to create more saliva and alleviate their oral discomfort.

⬆ When you see someone with a clenched jaw, and you can actually see the muscles on the sides of the jaw pulsate, you know that he is very angry. If he clenches his jaw and pulls it to the side, as you see here, he is extremely angry. He is basically doing what children and animals do naturally when they become angry—they bite. But because grown-ups are more mature and civilized and they understand the consequences of biting someone, the biting response instead occurs inside the person's mouth.

⬈ Anger can also be reflected in a chin jut, when someone aggressively sticks out his chin. The further the chin juts forth, the angrier the person and the greater the chance for a physical altercation. We see this chin jut with young children when they become defiant or assert their independence. And we see this facial gesture carried into adulthood when we have been wronged or are about to tell someone off.

✦When someone is afraid, you might see him tucking in his chin and recessing his jaw—he is "backing off" jaw-wise. The chin retracts much like a turtle retracts into its shell. So when you see someone recoil, pulling the head back and placing the chin on the neck, he is expressing fear.

✦People who rub their chin are displaying confusion or thinking about something and trying to come up with an idea, make a decision, or find a solution by calming themselves through self-soothing chin strokes. You often see chin stroking by those who are being critical of you, disapprove of what you have done, or simply don't trust you or what you are saying. They are processing what you told or didn't tell them, sitting in judgment of you, and not believing what you have said.

If you see someone raise his head and nose up in the air, he may be judging you or feeling superior.

Famed anthropologist Desmond Morris once said that you can learn a great deal about how people are really feeling by watching the activity in their lower facial region: the chin and jaw. You can tell whether they are angry, afraid, or even surprised based on the appearance of their jaws.

The Nose Knows

What a person does with her nose can reflect a range of feelings. If someone does not like what you said, you may see her lightly crinkle the bridge of her nose, similar to the expression she would make if something smelled bad. Her facial language says that what you have told or not told her is odious and offensive. You often see this expression on people who don't believe what they've just heard.

If someone is lying to you, the most common "tell" or signal is touching or pulling on the nose. When someone is not being truthful, the capillaries in the nose expand because of the increased blood flow and activity of the autonomic system. The sudden, minute physical changes in blood flow and the drying up of the mucosal membranes creates discomfort in the nasal area, which causes the person to itch and scratch.

Interestingly, the position of a person's nose can show how he feels about you. If you see someone raise his head and nose up in the air, he may be judging you or feeling superior. Conversely, when someone bows his head and you can see the bridge of his nose, as opposed to their nostrils, this may be a sign that he holds you in high esteem.

Body language involving the ear, like the nose, can indicate various emotions. Scratching behind the ear or cupping the ear can mean something different, such as the person doubted or wasn't sure about what you said. If you see this gesture, you may want to repeat yourself or elaborate on what you said. Another thing to look for when determining someone's interest is whether she continues to rub her ears between her thumb and forefinger or around the inner portion of her ear. If you see this, it may mean that she is bored with you, doesn't believe you, or doesn't want to hear your story.

One of the most common signs of deception is when someone touches or pulls on his nose.

↑When someone is attracted to you, you may see the sides of his nose slightly flare out as he speaks to you. Called the "nasal alar flare," it is nature's way of allowing him to absorb you not only visually but through the sense of smell. We emit pheromones, which others breathe in to determine whether they want to take the interaction further. If your pheromones are harmonious with another's and you begin a relationship, you will see this nasal flare, especially as he falls in love with you and the relationship progresses.

↑Just as scratching the nose may indicate that someone is lying, so does scratching the ear. It is not uncommon to see someone scratching, tugging, or pulling at his ear when confronted over his deception.

CHAPTER 4

HOW TO INTERPRET THE VOICE

THE GREEK PHILOSOPHER GALEN ONCE SAID, "It is the voice that mirrors the soul." And it's true that the sound of people's voices can tell you much about them. The pitch, loudness or softness, speed at which they speak, choppiness or fluidity, whether they attack their sounds with sudden bursts or trail off at the end of sentences, whether they speak in a monotone or variety of tones, or sound gravelly or sugar sweet tells you a tremendous amount about their personality and state of mind.

The voice is a barometer of how you feel about yourself and the world around you because what you are thinking and feeling emerges through the tone of your voice. You read a person's voice all the time without even realizing it. When someone you know well calls on the phone, you can easily tell whether he is in a good or bad mood. If it's your boss, you know whether something is wrong or not. In fact, we can pick up on most people's emotional states with a great deal of accuracy simply by listening to their voice.

As we hear a person speak and process what she has said and how she has said it through our auditory cortex, the information then filters through our limbic system, which controls our emotions. We in turn mirror or react to the emotion expressed through that voice.

Think of the voice as a conduit to what someone is thinking. When you tell someone great news and he replies in a monotone, "That's nice, I'm happy for you," chances are he is not happy for you as you hear no indication of a happy tone in his voice.

As my doctoral dissertation at the University of Minnesota revealed, a person's voice has a great effect on how he is perceived by others. If you have a pleasant-sounding voice, others will perceive you as more attractive, no matter how you look. Conversely, studies have shown that those who were initially perceived as attractive were subsequently perceived as being unattractive based on the way they sound. You have probably experienced this when you meet an attractive person only to be suddenly turned off after you hear them speak.

Use Caution When Doing Vocal Analysis!

Before you analyze a person's voice, know that there are neurological and physical problems that can account for aberrant vocal tones. For instance, when a person's voice sounds labored or shaky or it dies off at the end of sentences, it may not be nerves, stress, or deception at play. Instead, she could have Parkinson's disease or multiple sclerosis.

If someone sounds hyper-nasal, he may not be exhibiting laziness, sloppiness, or snobbery. Instead he could have a cleft palate or a neurological condition that causes him to sound nasal. If he mispronounces sounds that include the letter r or s, he may be deaf or hard of hearing. If he lisps, he may have a dental problem. If he speaks too loudly or too softly, he may have a specific type of hearing loss. If he sounds breathy or dies off at the end of sentences, he may have a respiratory or cardiac problem. If he chokes off his sounds, he may suffer from a vocal cord problem called spastic dysphonia. A high-pitched voice or chronically hoarse voice may be the result of trauma to the larynx or voice box. And finally, a person may sound slurred and die off at the end of sentences because he is on medications or using drugs.

Whether you are male or female, a high-pitched voice is associated with being immature, tentative, weak, or insecure.

What Qualities Make a Winning Voice?

People who enthusiastically use a lively, bouncy tone and varying inflection to express their emotions have winning voices. The pitch is both lower for men and women who have winning voices, and they speak in consistent, well-modulated tones that are appropriate for the situation. They don't speak too loudly or too softly.

The richness and resonance of their clear tones make them sound confident. Likewise, their vocal enthusiasm attracts others to them because they are perceived as being happy, positive individuals. People with a winning voice quality are listened to more often than those who do not have these positive voice characteristics as they tend to hold their audience's attention and are perceived as being intelligent and knowledgeable.

How We Perceive Voice Pitch

Whether you are male or female, a high-pitched voice is associated with being immature, tentative, weak, or insecure. There is also a sexual component to a high-pitched voice as the voice usually drops when a person is sexually aroused. A person with a high-pitched voice may be perceived as being nonsexual or in denial of his or her sexuality.

Suffering emotional trauma, such as being molested at a young age, can also explain a high-pitched voice. Psychiatrists have reported that emotional growth can be stifled by childhood trauma, when they became stuck and failed to evolve vocally. In my own practice, I have treated countless men and women with high-pitched voices who, as it turned out, had been emotionally and sexually abused as children.

People with higher pitched voices tend to be nervous, tense, and even angry. Research shows that when a person is angry, the pitch of her voice rises. It therefore stands to reason that if someone constantly speaks in a high-pitched voice, she may harbor internal anger or fear.

A vocal pattern related to pitch that is more common in women than men is when the pitch goes up at the end of sentences, making every statement sound as though the person is asking a question. This pattern projects tentativeness, insecurity, and a lack of confidence. It may also be a generational quirk meant to sound "cool." If someone speaks that way to gain peer acceptance, it is a clear sign of insecurity.

Although it is generally more pleasing to hear a lower rather than a higher tone, an excessively lowered voice indicates insecurity. It usually occurs in young men who erroneously believe that if they speak loudly at a low pitch, people will respect them and take them more seriously. But this actually has the opposite effect: Others tend to view them as insecure, phony, and trying too hard to impress.

Soft and Loud Voices

People who speak too quietly, forcing others to constantly ask them to speak up, enjoy the attention. They tend to have a passive-aggressive personality trait as they manipulate others to focus on them in a type of power play. By speaking in hushed tones, they succeed in gaining control over others in a sneaky way.

Soft talkers often harbor inner anger, which causes them to unexpectedly fly off the handle. In place of their quiet-as-a-mouse voice, you are suddenly confronted with a loud, booming tone filled with excess anger they have stored up for a long time.

Loud talkers also crave attention, but they go about getting it in a different way. By speaking loudly, they vocally impose themselves upon you. These types tend to be arrogant, pompous, controlling, competitive, bullying, and most of all, socially unconscious, unaware, or indifferent to social norms and what constitutes appropriate behavior.

Unless they have a specific type of hearing loss—a conductive hearing loss—their loud tones spring from the desire to be noticed because of a deep insecurity and lack of self-esteem.

Fading Out at the End of Sentences

People with this type of vocal pattern also suffer from low self-esteem. Unlike soft talkers, they don't usually use this pattern on purpose to manipulate others into paying attention to them. Instead, this vocal pattern is the product of sloppiness, laziness, a lack of control, or a lack of preciseness.

People who speak too quietly, forcing others to constantly ask them to speak up, enjoy the attention.

If they don't follow through with their tone to the end of a sentence, chances are they don't follow through in other areas of their lives. In my practice of listening to thousands of clients, I have found this to be the case. They are the type of person who frequently starts things and never finishes them.

Shaky Voice

Those with a tremor in their tone are usually upset, fearful, or nervous. They, too, can suffer from low self-worth and they tend to be nervous when talking to others. They often have a fear of being judged and spend a great deal of time concerned about what others think of them.

People with this type of voice are often tentative and have problems making decisions. They are hesitant to jump into something because they are worried about the repercussions of their actions. They tend to be overly concerned with who said what to whom and what was said about them. They live in the future, not the present, as they fear confronting their issues each day. In essence, they live on shaky ground, which is reflected in their shaky voice quality.

You should note that in addition to certain neurological conditions, specific types of psychotropic medications can cause the user's voice to become shaky. A shaky-sounding voice, therefore, may indicate that the speaker is being medically treated for a psychiatric problem, most likely related to mood stability.

Vocal Attackers and Nasal Whiners

Those who infuse their tones with bursts of loudness are often angry, aggressive, and competitive. They pepper their conversations with these attacking tones, which makes it jarring to listen to them. These tones are the equivalent of little shocks of hostility or blasts of hate and anger.

Competitive people such as these always seem to be looking for ways to top others during a conversation. They level criticism at others as reflected in these attacking tones, in an effort to feel and appear superior.

People with harsh, gravelly voices are angry and highly aggressive people. They tend to be bullying, demanding, and controlling. They use their tone to intimidate others as a way to gain both attention and power. This personality type often has its roots in childhood. Think back to the school bully when you were growing up—chances are they spoke in a harsh, angry tone of voice.

In a Gallup Poll commissioned more than two decades ago, it was discovered that most people are turned off by a nasal-sounding voice. This data still holds true. More than 70 percent found this voice quality to be annoying. Nasal whiners tend to complain and are highly critical of others and everything else around them, all of which is reflected in their dissatisfied tone. They regularly seem to be on the defensive.

Frenetic, Manic Tones

It is one thing to be cheery, optimistic, and upbeat, but when someone's tones don't make sense or have an inappropriate sense of urgency or alarm, there is something wrong with that person.

This type of tonal quality is often found in those who suffer from various psychiatric illnesses, especially bipolar disorder, which includes a manic phase. This kind of rapid-fire, forceful speaking pattern is called "pressured speech."

WHAT A DELIBERATELY SEXY, BREATHY TONE MEANS

People who speak in a breathy tone are trying to use their sexuality to get what they want. They are usually insecure as they use this ploy to make others think of them in sexual terms. Because they constantly communicate sex through their voice, it is not uncommon to discover that they harbor sexual issues or problems.

Researchers have found that those with breathy voices are not taken seriously and perceived as being untrustworthy. They often have an overinflated ego and feel entitled as they attempt to seduce others for their own personal gain, sexual or otherwise.

But there are those who communicate with this tone all the time. When you hear someone using bullet-like, roller-coaster tones to convey extreme excitement, turmoil, or crisis, that person is trying to manipulate you into helping him, financially or in another way. This type tends to be selfish, angry, overbearing, and dismissive of boundaries because they demand to be the center of attention. Whatever you communicate to them, rest assured that the topic will be redirected to their problem, issue, or crisis. They cannot be compassionate or sensitive to your needs because everything is always about them.

With manic speakers, it can be exciting to be around their high energy, but there is often no substance behind it. Never allow yourself to be drawn into their schemes or drama because it probably will not end up being in your best emotional or financial interest.

Rapid-Fire Talkers

Those with manic tones often use a variety of inflections, which makes their speech seem animated and exciting. In contrast, people with rapid-fire speech patterns often have a monotone and staccato-like sound that makes it seem as though they are vocally attacking you.

People who speak at an extremely rapid rate may be nervous, anxious, angry, or insecure. They subconsciously want to hurry up, get it all out, and get it over with because, deep down, they believe that others aren't interested in what they have to say. If they had more confidence, they would take the time to allow others to hear what they have to communicate.

They often tend to be type A personalities who are highly driven, aggressive, and ambitious. They are usually in a hurry and make others feel anxious and uncomfortable when listening to their rapid patter.

It is not uncommon for fast talkers to come from large families where competition to be heard is high. They have much in common with the loud talker who needs to be heard above the noise of other siblings. Fast talkers feel they have to speak faster to get everything out before they are interrupted.

Research has shown that fast talkers tend to exhibit more inner anger. A reason for this may be that because certain environments, such as densely populated cities or large families, in which there is competition for attention, tend to generate more stress and anger than other environments. As a result, people in these settings develop a rapid rate of speaking.

People who speak at an extremely rapid rate subconsciously want to hurry up, get it all out, and get it over with because, deep down, they believe that others aren't interested in what they have to say.

What Different Tones Can Indicate

People who speak in agitated tones are often accused of "copping an attitude," which in turn makes others hostile toward them. Their tones cause others to fight back as they respond to the person's verbal chip on their shoulder. They are highly critical and judgmental as they express their annoyance with you. If they don't like what someone does or says, they tend to take it personally. They believe everyone else is wrong and theirs is the only correct view.

The verbal fire burning within them ignites and shoots off flames through their tones, harming everyone in their path as they are so filled with inner rage that is difficult to quench.

Those who overarticulate or speak in choppy, deliberate tones tend to be headstrong, self-righteous, and inflexible. They find it difficult to bend and compromise. They are reminiscent of an admonishing grade-school teacher who speaks to a naughty child in short, simple sentences and exaggerated pronunciation.

On the other hand, those who speak in a monotone are usually not in touch with their emotions as they keep an emotional distance from others to avoid getting too close or hurt. This way of speaking also prevents others from getting close to them. These vocally ungenerous people often don't want you to know their true feelings and fear being found out, so they use noncommittal tones to keep others at bay.

Speaking with them can be frustrating and exhausting because they don't give you any feedback that allows you to react to their true thoughts and feelings and, in turn, have a genuine conversation. As a result, it is not uncommon for you to become angry when speaking to them and for others to perceive them as sneaky and withholding of information.

Because it is difficult for people who speak in a monotone to get their true intentions across, communicating with them tends to be a superficial exercise. Consequently, there can also be a great deal of miscommunication, misunderstanding, and mistrust as you never really know what they mean by what they say.

A monotone voice may also suggest that the person is depressed or harbors some inner sadness. And if they always sound like this, they may suffer from chronic depression.

Slow and Deliberate Tones

Like those who speak too fast, those who speak too slowly are often unconscious of others' feelings and how annoying it is to them. I am not talking about people with Southern accents who draw out their words or phrases, or those with a neuromotor condition involving nerve impulses that cause slow and labored speech, or those using medications that inhibit speech flow.

I am talking about people who, like the too-soft speaker, deliberately take their time drawing out their vowels to make sure they are being heard. Their slowness manipulates others by forcing them to hang on what they have to say.

If you try to interrupt them or hurry them along, they will usually ignore you and continue to speak over you. They will also ignore your annoyed body language as they insist on finishing their message. By doing so, they are on an aggressively rude and hostile power trip, indifferent to basic and polite human interaction.

There is, however, one exception to this pattern of behavior. Although the majority of this type of speaker tends to be self-absorbed, studies on emotion and rate of speech have shown that slow and deliberate speech can also be associated with sadness.

FLEE FROM SUGARY-SWEET TONES

No one is nice, happy, and cheery all the time. If you hear someone who continually sounds this way—run. Run as fast as you can and as far away as possible. Most often these people are highly passive-aggressive and angry. Their chronic sugary sweetness is only a mask that hides how they really feel. They are often sneaky and use their sweet tones to gather information from others and turn it against them, or they use the information for their own benefit.

People with this type of voice can turn on you in a moment's notice. Thus, it is essential to be aware of when their sugar kettle is about to boil over and to pay close attention to any double messages and incongruent behaviors where the actions don't match the words. When they do let out their repressed anger, it will explode in a barrage of vitriol, turning their sugary voice into acid tones.

CHAPTER 5

HOW TO READ SPEECH PATTERNS AND CONTENT

THE FOURTH AND FINAL ASPECT of accurately reading people involves paying attention to their speech patterns and content. Too often we gloss over what someone says only to be surprised later when they do something egregious. Had we really listened to exactly what they said, we would have known what to expect.

For instance, when people like you, they speak nicely to you. They are polite and considerate in what they say. They tell you the truth, and if they have to tell you something unpleasant, they do it in a kind and gentle way that doesn't destroy your feelings. They really listen to what you have to say and respond accordingly. They realize the conversation isn't always about them, and they don't need to take center stage. Because they are emotionally secure, they view communication as a form of give and take in which they relay understanding and compassion.

Unfortunately, there are too many people who are insecure, which leads them to say things that have double meanings or are hurtful. In this chapter, we will see what they really mean by what they say.

When Words Hurt

If someone cuts you down and then tells you she was only kidding, rest assured she was not. These kidders and teasers may claim they are just having fun, but they are doing so at your expense. They are the type of person who doesn't confront anger head on. Instead, they do it in a roundabout way through humor. In essence, they have hidden anger or jealousy toward you, and they show it by poking fun at you. Sarcasm hurts. It is disguised hostility.

Then there are the "verbally unconscious"—people who constantly put their foot in their mouth by using outdated words or politically incorrect terms. It is as though they are in a time warp and not aware that times have changed, and they inadvertently say things they don't realize may be hurtful to you.

Most often, these types of people mean no harm, they are just unaware. When you point out that your feelings were hurt by what they said, they will typically be very apologetic, unlike the person who is too blunt. Although we are not discussing pathologies in this book, it is important to note that those with Asperger's syndrome often don't realize that what they are saying to someone may be hurtful. That is why it is important to point out to others whenever their words hurt you.

Unfortunately, there are people whose conscious aim is to hurt others. These people are like verbal bulls in a china shop. They are well aware of how their words hurt and sting others, and they do it for some type of sadistic thrill. When you tell them they are being hurtful, they may laugh, ignore what you've said, or tell you to get over it. They are verbal bullies whose goal is to intimidate, humiliate, and alienate.

Then there are people who, no matter what you say, say the opposite. If you say "yes," these verbal bullies will say "no" just for the sake of contradicting you and letting you know they don't respect you. Their objective is to verbally take you down a notch. Their actions tell you that they feel competitive with you and are intimidated or threatened by you.

The Chatterbox

They won't shut up. They talk and talk without a filter. People like this are often lonely and insecure, need a lot of attention, and want to be liked. They only feel comfortable when they hear the sound of their own voice. They are similar to the verbally unconscious in that they are rarely aware of how their constant chatter annoys others. Sometimes they talk nonstop because it calms their inner anxiety.

Because they have no boundaries, they will give you way too much information about themselves, and, like children, they see nothing wrong with it. They are unconcerned that divulging their most intimate secrets may subject them to ridicule or come back to haunt them. Their main concern is to talk it all out.

Gossiper/Nosybody

Though it is human nature to enjoy a good piece of gossip, people who focus most of their time uncovering and transferring information to others have no life of their own. They are in everyone's business because they have no business of their own.

They speak ill of others to gain power and feel better about themselves. In reality, they are insecure and envious of the lives of others. They are competitive and intrusive. They appear to be stuck at the maturity level of young children who tend to ask personal questions that may not be appropriate, such as, "When are you having a baby?" They are curious, so they ask, regardless of whether the question is rude or invasive. Then they offer their unsolicited opinion and share what you told them with everyone else because they have no boundaries, censor, or withholding capability.

The Liar or Exaggerator

People lie for a number of reasons. They may lie out of a sense of hostility because they don't want you to know what is going on in their life; they are very self-protective and may have something to hide. They lie or exaggerate the truth to feel better about themselves and to look better in the eyes of others, in which case, they are lying out of a sense of insecurity. Sometimes

THE ME, MYSELF, AND I SYNDROME

When people constantly talk about themselves, it's a sure sign of insecurity. When they apply everything you say back to them, they reveal their envy. No matter how many stories they relay about themselves, there is no spotlight big enough for them. This behavior points to an obvious void in their early childhood development. Perhaps they were abused or didn't get enough attention. It is as if they are stuck in a childhood phase when the whole world seemed to revolve around them and their needs. The constant bragging is their attempt to repair their severely shattered self-esteem. Many perceive them as arrogant, self-absorbed, or snobby, but their underlying issue is a deep-rooted insecurity.

Insecurity can reveal itself in other ways, such as, for instance, people who tear themselves down before anyone else does. Their need for approval is so great that they feel if they poke fun at themselves, no one else will, and they will be liked. They tell you what is wrong with them and readily divulge all their weaknesses in an attempt to gain support and sympathy. They share many traits with the "Me, Myself, and I Syndrome" in that they are terribly insecure and need to constantly focus on themselves. The only difference is that what they reveal about themselves tends to be negative.

Then there are those who are afraid to make waves or offend anyone. So they play it safe by refusing to take a stand and saying instead that they don't know. They tend to be quiet people who are wishy-washy in their beliefs. They can go either way, depending on the crowd. These verbally stingy people are highly insecure.

A person known for being quiet can indicate a number of motivations. Some people don't want to appear stupid or ignorant so they choose to say nothing. They may also be painfully shy and insecure, so they give minimal answers, which are oftentimes one-word responses, such as "yep" or "nope." They may also be antisocial people who avoid others. Or they may be selfish and more interested in getting information than giving it. So they keep quiet and absorb all the information without revealing anything about themselves, and you never know where they stand on any issue.

You can often spot liars by what they say. They tend to wander verbally as they get to the point.

people lie because they are bored and want to stir things up and make them sound more interesting. Others may lie to be polite and avoid hurting someone's feelings.

You can often spot liars by what they say. They tend to wander verbally as they get to the point, going off on tangents and side stories as a way to mask their lies. Listen carefully and you will notice them making a slip of the tongue in which they betray themselves by revealing significant information, and then they will immediately try to correct their error.

Liars are often highly complementary toward you. When people do this, chances are they don't like you as much as they want you to believe or they want something from you. As Confucius said in 500 BCE, "Never trust a person who is fawning." In addition, they tend to answer a question with a question and repeat the exact words you said to them.

Liars commonly stammer or hesitate over crucial information. (Of course, not everyone who stutters or hesitates is a liar. Some people stutter because of speech problems or neurological issues.) They will speak in disjointed fragments that don't make sense, especially when they are confronted with questions or caught in a lie. Here I am talking specifically about someone who is normally fluid in their speech pattern and suddenly stammers when discussing a crucial point or asked a significant question.

The Constant Complainer

When people constantly complain about others, they do it to feel superior because deep down they feel badly about themselves. It is a sign of profound insecurity.

People who constantly complain about themselves, their ailments, family, or work usually do so to gain attention. They do it as a way to bond with others and obtain both attention and sympathy. What they don't realize is that their constant complaining usually has the opposite effect because eventually no one wants to be around them. They are highly critical and judgmental of others because they fear being criticized and judged.

Those Who Curse and Use Slang

Many people pepper their speech with curse words for their shock value or because they feel it makes them sound tough or cool or part of a specific group. In other instances, using foul language can be a defense mechanism to keep people at bay. Bullies and control freaks often use curse words as an attention-getting device or to prove their dominance over others.

Similarly, people who use ethnic flavoring when speaking to someone belonging to that ethnic group do so to create a bond and feel like they are a member of the group or to appear cool or important.

PART 2

DECIPHERING WHAT IT ALL MEANS

CHAPTER 6

UNDERSTANDING THE BODY LANGUAGE OF THE SEXES TO PREVENT MISUNDERSTANDINGS

MEN AND WOMEN COMMUNICATE and use body language that can be confusing to one another, which can lead to negative feelings and misunderstandings.

One of the main differences between men and women involves space and distance. Men take up more physical room and space than women as they spread their limbs out during business and social interactions. This behavior can create problems on a social level.

↑Men typically take up more space than women, spreading out their limbs, work items, and so on, which can cause confusion and misunderstanding between the sexes.

Let's say a man and woman are on a first date. They are seated on a couch when suddenly he spreads his legs apart and drapes his arm over the top of the couch, in typical male territorial body language. The woman, in turn, may interpret this behavior as rude or an attempt to hog the couch as she is relegated to the corner, her arms and hands at her sides or hands folded on her lap.

If she is just getting to know the guy or isn't interested in him, this kind of action can create discomfort and even animosity. She may misinterpret his arm draped on the top of the couch as an attempt to be too forward or pushy.

Men also have a tendency to point their fingers when they speak, making them appear more aggressive, while women tend to find any form of finger-pointing condescending.

↑Men tend to take up more space when gesturing, which may incorrectly convey aggression. And in general, men make larger and more sweeping gestures away from, rather than toward, their body.

↑Women tend to do the opposite, using smaller gestures and employing a more curved hand movement.

When men are seated and listening to someone, they tend to lean back in a reclining position, interlock their fingers behind their neck, and fidget. A woman may misconstrue these behaviors to mean the man isn't taking what she has to say seriously, is being inattentive, or doesn't care or think what she has to say is important. Instead, it is simply a typical male sitting and listening body language position. Inattention, on the other hand, is when someone doesn't look at you or ignores you.

Women tend to lean directly forward when listening, which makes them appear more attentive.

✦ Whether because of the culture of men engaged in team sports where bodily contact is the norm or male bonding, in which back slapping, patting, and touching are signs of camaraderie, men tend to touch other men and women more when speaking. Studies show that they touch women more when guiding them through a door or assisting them with their coats.

Men, more than women, tend to touch others when speaking. Women can easily misinterpret this behavior as flirting, when that may not be the intention at all. In a work environment, where sexual harassment is a serious concern, this typical male touching behavior can be particularly problematic.

Men may also create problems for themselves professionally because they tend to invade other people's personal space by sometimes standing too close to them. In contrast, women are inclined to keep a greater distance as they approach others, thereby encroaching less on their physical space.

Gender Difference Misinterpretations in Facial Language

A major facial language difference between men and women is that men sometimes tend to avoid eye contact and not look directly at the other person with whom they are speaking. Instead, they look at the other person from an angle. Women, on the other hand, tend to look directly at the person they're speaking to.

As a result of these differing communication styles, it is not unusual for a woman to feel as though the man isn't attentive or closely listening to and absorbing everything she has to say.

Even during a positive interaction, confusion may arise because men use little direct eye contact. If a couple is talking about their relationship, for instance, and the man isn't looking directly at the woman, she may have doubt his sincerity and how he really feels about her.

This disparate facial language between men and women can cause a great deal of confusion on both sides. When a women smiles and nods as she listens, it does not necessarily mean that she agrees with or likes what is being said. It may mean that she is being polite and encouraging the speaker to continue. And women may misinterpret the male tendency to frown and squint while listening as anger, displeasure, or disagreement with what is being said.

In addition, men are inclined to provide fewer reactions and less feedback, while women react more and convey greater emotional warmth through their facial expressions. Women also tend to use more jaw movement and more precise articulation when speaking while men do not open their jaws as much, thereby creating less facial movement.

Communication Differences during Negative and Positive Interactions

Whether in the animal or human kingdom, when eye contact is maintained, it signifies control or power over a situation and establishes dominance over the other animal or person. Breaking eye contact suggests submissiveness. There could be a misunderstanding on the man's part when he notices the woman averting her eyes. He may wrongly believe that he "won" the argument and that she backed down. This may not be the case at all. She may simply be doing what is common in female facial language.

In addition to facial differences, men and women differ with respect to voice tones. Studies show that men often use three tones while speaking, whereas women typically use five. This variation makes men sound less emotional than women, when this may not be the case. Women may therefore mistake a man's three-tone range as not being sensitive or emotional when it's simply a gender difference.

Because men use fewer tones, their inflection is more limited when they try to emphasize a point. So they may raise the volume of their voice for emphasis, which could give the erroneous impression that they are angry.

In contrast, women tend to speak less loudly than men. Women may speak in a soft voice with higher pitches in an attempt to appear sexy and feminine. They also phrase declarative statements as though they are asking a question, which makes them sound tentative. For instance, instead of saying, "It's two o'clock," using a downward inflection, they will say, "It's two o'clock?" using an upward inflection. If a woman uses this upward inflection throughout a conversation, she may cause the listener to doubt what she is saying and take her words less seriously.

For many men, it is difficult to take a woman who speaks in this volume and vocal tone and with this inflection pattern seriously. In fact, according to research, they may perceive the woman as neither intelligent nor competent, when it is not true.

↖ Men make less eye contact than women during conversations, which can be misinterpreted as boredom or lack of interest.

← When listening, women tend to smile, nod their head "yes," and appear more agreeable than men. Men often exhibit the opposite facial expression, frowning and squinting, when listening to others.

Speech and Voice Issues

A major speech difference between the sexes is that men interrupt more than women. Studies show that 73 to 93 percent of the interruptions during a conversation are made by men. This conversational style, which can be extremely annoying, can easily be misconstrued by the person being interrupted. The woman may think the man is rude and obnoxious when he is neither; he's simply exhibiting characteristics that are common to his gender.

Men also speak in a louder tone and in a more monotonous, less inflected voice than women, which may give the wrong impression that they are angry, bored, or disinterested. Similarly, the fact that men tend to speak in more staccato, choppy-sounding tones may make them sound abrupt and unapproachable to a woman.

Men have also been shown to disclose less personal information about themselves up front than women, which may give the impression that they are closed off or not friendly or approachable. For her part, because a woman tends to divulge more personal details early on in a conversation, she may be perceived by a man as sharing too much information.

Speaking in Direct Versus Indirect Terms

Another major speech difference between the genders is that men tend to speak more directly than women, who may interpret these statements as signs that he is hostile, controlling, angry, or accusatory. For example, he may say, "You didn't call." The woman, on the other hand, will make more accusations such as "Why didn't you call?" which can and often does give the man the erroneous impression that she is nagging him.

Another reason why women may be perceived as naggers may be their tendency to make more compound requests, such as, "Please go and help get the groceries, and while you are out there, can you get my sweater and red glasses that I left in the car?" Men, on the other hand, make simpler, single-task requests.

⬉ During a negative interaction, men will usually stare and maintain eye contact, visually focusing on the person with whom they are in conflict.

⬅ During an argument, women often lower their eyes and avert their gaze. In general, women are more likely than men to avoid confrontation and anger.

Getting to the Point

The number-one complaint that men report when communicating with the opposite sex is that women don't get to the point quickly enough. They feel that women use flowery and indirect language as opposed to being direct. This is even more evident when the woman has to discuss something that she considers unpleasant. Men are less verbose and are more direct in their approach.

As a result, many women feel that men are closed off when it comes to communicating and that they refuse to open up. This may be because men tend to be more silent during the conversation; they raise fewer topics of conversation; they use fewer intensifiers such as "few," "so," "very," "really," and "much"; and they use fewer psychological— or emotional—state verbs such as "I hope" or "I feel," preferring to answer questions with more objective terms.

In addition, men can sometimes use more teasing and sarcasm to show affection, whereas women generally offer more compliments and praise.

Men have a tendency to speak in monologues when expressing themselves, which can sound like they are lecturing or talking at you, as opposed to with you. In contrast, women's conversations resemble a dialogue in which there is more give-and-take. It is easy to see how these two distinct communication styles can cause a great deal of frustration—both for the woman who may feel she is being ignored and for the man who may feel he is being interrupted and minimized.

Because men are socialized to make more direct requests for what they want and women are conditioned to be accommodating and less direct, women often expect men to know automatically what they want without actually telling them. A woman will hint at what she wants instead of being direct, which leads to the man being confused.

Differences in Arguing and Apologizing

Men view arguments as having a beginning, a middle, and an end. When they are over, most men don't hold grudges or bring things up from the past. Women, however, see arguments as continuing over time, and they think nothing of bringing up incidents from years earlier, which can be confusing for men. Women also tend to hold grudges more often and for longer periods, which makes it difficult to incorporate men's "forgive-and-forget" approach.

Moreover, women take what they perceive as verbal rejection more personally while men minimize it and can more easily let it go.

Men view arguments as having a beginning, a middle, and an end. Women, however, see arguments as continuing over time.

Men apologize less while women apologize for things that have nothing to do with them. When men do apologize, they are more embarrassed but use less emotion, which can give the wrong impression that they aren't genuinely sorry or the apology is insincere.

Ego Confusion

Women are brought up to refrain from bragging and to be modest about their accomplishments while focusing more on the achievements of others. Consequently, they are less comfortable than men when receiving accolades.

Men, on the other hand, are conditioned since childhood to talk about themselves and their achievements: the more the man accomplishes and achieves, the more money he makes, or the more protective and stronger he appears, which he believes makes him a better provider and more desirable mate. From their perspective, women may look at this behavior as boasting, showing off, or being ego-driven and self-absorbed, when it is not necessarily the case.

When Conversation Differences Cause Confusion

When women converse, they enjoy the minute details of a story, which can be irritating to many men who just want to get to the bottom line. They become frustrated when women go off on a tangent as they tell a story or follow a stream of consciousness that doesn't have a beginning, middle, and end.

A woman interprets a man's not remembering the details of their first date as not caring or not being sensitive and romantic when that may not be the case. Unlike women, men don't process information in terms of details.

ASKING FOR HELP

Men are not conditioned to ask for help like women are—they are raised to figure things out on their own. This difference in social conditioning can be one of the most common misunderstandings when it comes to something like asking for directions.

Although many jokes have been made on the subject, there is nothing funny or more frustrating for a woman than wasting time driving around when it would be so easy to ask someone for directions instead of waiting for the man to figure it out.

Men and women also talk about different things. While women prefer to discuss personal issues, including relationships, men speak more objectively. Men also talk more about what they did, what they are going to do, and where they went. Women, on the other hand, talk more about how they feel about what they did and where they went. Thus it can feel to both sexes as if they can't relate to what the other is saying.

Problem-Solving

When a woman has a problem, she wants a man to commiserate with her. She wants his emotional support and validation. She doesn't want him necessarily to fix or solve the problem. The man, however, thinks he is doing her a favor by telling her what to do to resolve her issue. She in turn perceives his help as being controlling and bossy.

In contrast, when a woman hears a man's problem and offers no solution but instead shows him compassion and sympathy, it is easy to see why he might feel he is wasting his time because she is merely providing sympathy when he's looking for solutions.

When men feel stressed, upset, or uptight, they are likely to stop talking and chill out while they figure things out and regroup. Women do the opposite—they want to talk things out. So when a man does his thing and retreats, she may interpret it as his being upset with her and wonder what she did wrong and why he is shutting her out.

CHAPTER 7

HOW TO JUDGE THE STRENGTH OF YOUR ROMANTIC RELATIONSHIP

AS PART OF MY BODY LANGUAGE BUSINESS, I offer a service at drlillianglass.com where people can send me photos or videos of themselves and their mate or potential mate and ask me to analyze what I think of them and their relationship.

I do this for various media outlets as well because I am constantly asked to decipher the body language of celebrities and newsmakers. Television shows, magazines, and Internet sites want to know whether a star's relationship is genuine or an attempt by his or her handlers to create a public relations spin to keep their client relevant or to promote an upcoming film or television show.

If the relationship is for real, they want to know how the couple is doing. Are they still madly in love or is there a glitch in their relationship? Will they stay together or will they break up?

Just by analyzing the couple's body language, I have been very successful in predicting whose relationship is in trouble well before any formal separation gets announced in the press.

What to Look for If Someone Is into You

I look for a number of things to determine whether a couple likes each other, from the distance they stand, walk, or sit to each other to the position of their lips and jaws. I do this analysis with famous people, but by knowing what to look for, you can learn to do what I do and apply that knowledge when analyzing your own photos and videos and those of your loved ones. Some of what I look for includes:

- Smiles and other facial expressions
- Whether they look or don't look at each other; their eye position and movement
- Jaw and lip action, especially while kissing
- How they hug, how their hips are positioned, and the space and distance between them
- How they touch each other and whether there is muscle tension
- The way their feet are positioned near each other
- Positive and negative signs of sexual attraction and signs of affection or hostility
- Mirroring
- What their hands are doing
- Shoulder and chest positions

I'll describe these items in greater detail later in this book. The more photos I see, the more I can look for consistencies in their behavior toward each other. When I look at photos of the couple with other people or when they are standing or sitting alone, it helps me gain knowledge of the overall situation.

Videotape analyses are also excellent because I can look for leakage, when real feelings indicated by specific behaviors leak out, which tells me how the couple really feels about each other.

If you want to know whether someone is really into you, look at how he smiles at you. A smile that is genuine shows the person's teeth.

What a Smile Can Say

For centuries, people have been captivated by the smile on Da Vinci's Mona Lisa. It is actually a half-smile, which shows the woman's ambivalence as the left side of her face curves upward, suggesting a smile, while the right side remains neutral. If she were in a relationship, her facial language would tell us that she may not feel 100 percent committed. Though she may tell her lover that she loves him, her eyes, which shift to the side, indicate that she may not mean it. The puffiness under the sides of her nose and on top of her upper lip indicates tension, which further confirms her expression of ambivalence.

If you want to know whether someone is really into you, look at how he smiles at you. Is it a tight, forced smile or a half-smile with the lips pulled back tightly and not showing any teeth? If so, that person is uncertain about how he feels about you. If you have a photo of him smiling, cover his lips with your hands and you will notice that instead of smiling, he looks serious.

A smile that is genuine shows the person's teeth. The apples of their cheeks are raised and their lips are parted. If you cover their mouth in a photo, their eyes will be smiling. That is how you know the smile is real.

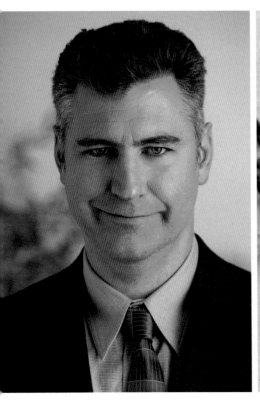

↑ A tight, forced smile or a half-smile with the lips pulled back tightly and not showing any teeth means that person is uncertain about how they feel about you.

↑ Even though this couple is smiling and leaning toward each other, upon closer inspection you will notice that the woman appears to be more into her man than he is into her. Her smile is genuine, with raised cheeks, smiling eyes, and lips parted to show her teeth. She leans her head into his head in a display of affection. He, in turn, wears an ambivalent smile with his lips pulled back tightly. His nonsmiling eyes express ambivalence about the relationship.

✦When someone likes you, he smiles a lot, his eyebrows are raised, and his eyes open wide. He hugs you like he means it. You both feel each other's body close to you because there is no physical space between you. He wants to engulf you and you feel the same. He has a genuine expression of joy on his face.

✦When someone is not into you, she can barely look at you, let alone touch you. She puts a great deal of space and distance between you. If someone is not wearing an expression of joy when she hugs you, the relationship is in trouble and on its way out.

↑ If you hug your partner and there is distance between you at the lower body level, chances are there is a lack of sexual attraction and physical chemistry between you.

↑There may be intimacy issues if a person always insists on hugging you from behind or insists on being in back of you.

↑Hugging, when there is genuine romantic affection and mutual attraction, takes place face to face, belly button to belly button.

✦ If one of the parties raises her shoulder and keeps her hands and arms to herself instead of touching the other, there is trouble in the relationship. When couples are into each other, they stay physically close and can't keep their hands and arms off of each other.

✦ If someone touches you at the shoulder area, she most likely just wants to be friends.

The Distance Someone Keeps from You

When someone likes you, she can't get close enough to you, whether she is sitting, standing, or walking near you. A couple that is into each other touches in some way, with their chests, hips, or arms, as they lean into each other. It shows sexual chemistry.

When someone is not into you, not only is there significant physical distance between you, but the person leans away. It is a subconscious message that she wants to leave and can't wait to get away from you. Leaning away is often accompanied by covering the body as a subconscious means of protection, such as folding the arms across the torso.

⬆ Couples who like each other not only lean toward each other, they also walk in sync as they are literally in step with each other. They would never think of walking in back of or in front of each other.

↑ If someone touches your arm below the elbow, she is probably interested in getting closer, and if she touches your thigh or lower body, she is very attracted to you.

↟Men may put both hands in their pockets, with their thumbs pointing towards their male organ. It is not meant to be vulgar, and most men don't consciously realize they are doing it. But when they are attracted to a woman, many men automatically make this gesture, especially in bars and clubs when they are trying to pick up women.

↟Women also showcase their bodies to show a man they are interested, but they do it differently. They will often play with a necklace to draw attention to their neck and breast area, which says they are available, vulnerable, and open. Fiddling with their jewelry draws attention to the area that attracts most men— the breasts. Similarly, women often toss their hair off their shoulders to draw attention to their upper body.

How a couple walks together is very revealing. A huge giveaway that a couple does not connect with each other is in how many steps separate them. When one half of a couple walks several paces in front of the other and leaves the other behind, it means that he or she doesn't respect the other person and is trying to distance him- or herself.

Even though men usually have a wider stride than women, there is never any excuse for a man to walk ahead of a woman. In Western culture, it shows rudeness and a lack of concern and respect.

If someone covers her body with her arms or hands, know that she wants you to stay away from her body. If you notice that her hands are cupped as she covers up, it means that she doesn't want you to touch her and that she is angry with you. Where a person touches you also tells you how that person feels about you.

Animals use their body language as they preen and show off their body parts to attract a mate. A peacock will display his feathers during mating season while a baboon may show off her bottom. The same thing occurs in the human kingdom.

↑ People attracted to each other lean into each other. It is a primitive behavior that allows for a closer view and closer smell.

Eye Contact and Mirroring

When people are interested in each other, they subconsciously do what the other person does. The reason they can tell what the other person is doing is because they constantly look at them. They are literally taking the person in, breathing in the person's smell with the sides of their nose flaring as they try to detect compatible pheromones. They also absorb the person visually as they subconsciously watch for mutual attraction, such as pupils widening and eyes becoming moist and attentive.

The reason why people who are attracted to each other have great eye contact is that they like what they see. They like observing the other person's appearance, movements, and nuances, which give off clues that they may be like-minded and that there may be a shared attraction.

After a while, when the couple feels more at ease because they have both subconsciously agreed that they like each other's smell and the pheromones they each give off and they discover that they find each other visually appealing, they begin to bond by mirroring each other's behaviors and nuances. It is the equivalent of saying, "I identify with you and I am just like you." When the mirroring is genuine, it happens automatically, and you aren't even aware of it. If you suddenly become aware of it, you may find it amusing.

← If you are sitting across from someone and notice that her toe is pointing up, there is a good chance that she is attracted to you because it signifies that she is happy. Toes pointing up indicate happiness, while toes pointing down, with the heel off the ground, indicate the opposite. If the person's toes point in your direction while you are sitting or standing, she likes you. If you see one of their feet positioned with their toes pointing toward the door or the buffet table, she either wants to leave or she wants to get some food.

Although books offering advice on finding a mate try to teach you how to manipulate others and have them like you by mirroring their movements, it doesn't work when the behavior is contrived. Mirroring is a natural phenomenon that occurs when two people are genuinely into each other, and it cannot be manufactured.

A Kiss Is Just a Kiss

A kiss is the ultimate test to validate whether your vision and sense of smell have deceived you. A kiss is your chance to get extremely close to see, smell, and taste the person who has attracted you. You may like their looks, but they may not smell or taste right to you and that will end the attraction.

When you are initially into a person and vice versa, you cannot stop kissing each other because all your senses are stimulated by them. But when a relationship wanes, it starts with the kiss. Kisses become perfunctory, short, and hard. They become hard because of lip tension that says, "I don't really want to be kissing you."

Kisses are supposed to be soft and moist, and when they are hard and dry, you can be sure that the person is not into you.

How Someone's Voice Reflects Attraction

When people like you, first and foremost they speak to you with respect. In addition, they do the following:

1. Speak in sweet-sounding, nonharsh tones

2. Speak with a lilt in their voice, conveying animation and excitement

← When someone is into you, that person laughs a lot with you.

3. Engage in give-and-take during conversations

4. Elaborate on what you say and ask questions—They relate their experiences to what you have just said

5. Sprinkle their speech with terms of endearment and politeness

6. Never think of putting you down or hurting your feelings in any way

7. Speak truthfully

8. Openly and readily discuss and clear up misunderstandings or miscommunications

9. Make definite future plans to see you again

10. Show interest in your plans, friends, and family

When people don't like you, they do the following

1. Answer abruptly, give curt answers to your questions, and do not elaborate

2. Don't reciprocate or ask you questions

3. Constantly talk about themselves

4. Exaggerate or lie to you

5. Are critical, judgmental, or sarcastic

6. Make it a point to put you down

7. Compete with you or try to top you to show they are better than you

8. Negate or minimize what you hold dear (career, family, friends, pets, hobbies, etc.)

✦ It's time to get out of the relationship when the other person rolls his or her eyes or makes faces when you speak, accompanied by an audible sigh of impatience and disgust. The eye-rolling and face-making doesn't just happen in private. It happens most of the time, especially when you are in the company of others.

When It's Time to Bail

Every relationship has its ups and downs, but there comes a time when the relationship can no longer continue. When the anger has escalated to the point where verbal and physical violence may erupt, it is time to call it quits. Here are several body language and speech and voice red flags that signal the end of a relationship:

- They constantly speak loudly and in an angry, impatient, and disgusted tone.

- They blame and are accusatory toward you.

- They call you names and curse at you.

- They demean and degrade you, telling you directly or indirectly that you are stupid, ugly, fat, etc.

- They compare you to others as they point out your flaws and shortcomings.

- The two of you no longer have civilized conversations, only arguments.

- They are physically in your face and in your space, ready for battle with their hands on their hips.

- They gnash their teeth in anger. These actions are often precursors to verbal and/or physical violence—warning you to leave.

- When someone points a finger in your face or at your chest, know that the next step is usually physical violence—You are in danger and need to leave the relationship. There is no going back because all respect has been lost.

CHAPTER 8

DETERMINING AND DEFINING YOUR POTENTIAL AS A JOB CANDIDATE

IF YOU WANT TO GET A JOB, keep your job, improve your business, or know whom you can trust, you must know how to read people. You must know what their body and facial language and voice and speech patterns are saying at all times. If you do, you will have the Body Language Advantage, which can and will translate into dollars and cents.

The first thing you need to know is whom you can trust. What do their body language, voice, and communication patterns say? Do your instincts tell you something just doesn't seem right? Are you picking up on something that makes you doubt their abilities or honesty? If you choose to ignore what you see and hear, it can adversely affect your business. No one can work with someone they cannot trust. If you are forced to do so, then you will feel compelled to monitor them constantly. To learn how to trust someone, the first person you need to trust is yourself and your instincts. In chapter 3, I shared how essential it is to learn and practice the techniques to develop your instincts and gut reactions to people. People raise warning signs through their body language. Never overlook these signs. Pay close attention and respond accordingly.

Unless there is something that instantly puts you on your guard when you first meet someone with whom you will be doing business, trust everyone until you have reason not to.

However, there are warning signs that should make you watch someone more carefully and reserve your trust in that person:

1. They talk too quickly, seem verbally slick, and their speech sounds rehearsed.
2. They insist you make a decision immediately without having time to mull things over.
3. They get angry when you don't respond as they would like and turn belligerent or into a bully when you say "no" to them.
4. They gossip to you about others.
5. They lie and cheat and take delight in bragging about their cleverness in manipulating or conning people.
6. They constantly tell you all about their woes with the aim of getting you to help them financially or otherwise.

If you notice these behaviors in a co-worker, boss, or employer, know that you are in the presence of someone toxic and you should act accordingly. You have many options for how to deal with them. By using the Body Language Advantage, you can figure out what they are up to and with whom you are dealing and avoid falling prey to their drama and schemes.

What Initial Introductions Can Tell You

In the business world, you can tell a lot about people in the first few seconds of meeting them, from their posture and the way they carry themselves, to how they speak, to how they shake your hand and how far they stand from you when they shake it.

✦You may see people dusting off or brushing their shoulders with their hands as though they are grooming themselves. This may indicate deception during crucial questioning as though they are literally brushing away a lie. This grooming behavior, when there is no lint to be brushed off, is commonly seen when someone is attempting to deceive. It is usually first seen at the shoulders and continues down the body as you see the person systematically dust off his arms, torso, lap, and legs. It may also reflect a person's insecurity.

✦When someone keeps their distance from you when they shake your hand, that is exactly what they are doing—keeping a distance. They either don't like you or are intimidated by you. If it happens on your initial meeting, you can chalk it up to nerves or that the person doesn't know you yet. But if they give you a distant shake at the end of a meeting, rest assured that you most likely will not be getting along or doing business together.

As soon as someone sits down to interview you, you will have an inkling as to whether he likes you. The main tell is whether he looks at you. If not, chances are he is preoccupied with something else and doesn't want to waste time interviewing you, or he simply doesn't like you. If it is the latter and you have tried every which way to be pleasant, to bond with him, and to say what you think he might like to hear and it is still not working, sit back, relax, and smile. Say little unless you are asked a question. In other words, you didn't get the job.

Here are other clues that say you won't be working for nor doing business with that company or organization because the interview has gone south:

- She takes calls or continually allows others in and out her office during your interview.
- She does other work as you sit there, and she speaks to you in an annoyed tone.
- She talks about herself and her accomplishments and asks few questions about you.
- She is contentious and argues with whatever you say.
- She is belittling, sarcastic, or condescending during your meeting.
- She speaks to you in loud, harsh, or curt tones.
- She backs away from you when you speak.
- The interview ends abruptly without a term of politeness or any reference to future meetings.

How to Know Your Interview Went Well

Although it would be wonderful to be able to look for certain signs that mean you got the job, the process just doesn't work that way. A job interview can go perfectly, and then someone's less-qualified girlfriend or cousin or college buddy gets the job instead of you. But there are definite indicators that tell you the interview went well from a body language standpoint:

1. They look at you and smile during most of the interview.
2. They are pleasant and polite.
3. They lean in when speaking to you, are attentive, and nod when you speak.
4. They don't allow others to interrupt your meeting, and they speak to you respectfully.
5. They tell you a lot about the company or organization and discuss how you may fit in.
6. They introduce you to other key people in the company or organization.
7. When you leave, they assure you that they will be in touch.

↑ If you notice their forehead wrinkling with a crease in the middle above the nasal bridge, they don't believe you. It is therefore important for you to explain yourself further so they get your point.

↑ During business meetings, pay close attention to a person's hands. You will see their open palms if they are being open, honest, and forthright.

Body Language Tells in Business

When you are in an interview or having a business meeting and you notice the other person tilt or cock his head to the side, know that he is either not processing what you said, isn't sure of what you said, or doesn't believe what you said.

＋When his palms are down or turned to the side, that person may not be telling the whole story or may not believe what he himself is saying. He may be holding back important information or he may be less than forthright with you.

→When people speak to you and their hand is straight-forward, fingers held tightly together, and they make small karate choplike movements when they speak, it means they are emphatic about what they are saying. It will be difficult to change their mind because they are extremely committed to their point of view.

⬆If someone crosses her arms under the breasts or chest, above the abdomen, it may mean that she is chilly or just resting her arms on her tummy (something often seen with pregnant women).

What Arms and Hand Gestures Can Mean

Just because someone crosses her arms, it doesn't mean that she is closing herself off to you or shutting you out. It depends on a number of things, such as the location of the arms in relation to the body.

If there is no muscle tension in the fingers as she does this, it is a good sign. It only becomes a bad sign when you see her tensing up and squeezing her forearm. In that case, it can mean stress, tension, or conflict. This is why it is so important to consider the context of the situation and additional details, such as the appearance of muscle tension and what the facial language is saying.

As I said earlier, when people lift their hands toward their face and touch each of their fingers together, it is called steepling. It can mean that the person is carefully listening to and analyzing you. In a business setting, it is a gesture that conveys power. It says that the person is thinking and judging what you are saying and doing. It says that he is in control.

The Spaces Around and In-Between

When a person takes up a lot of room and spreads his work out in a meeting, it means he is showing confidence and asserting his power. Although men tend to do this more often than women, when you observe a woman doing it, she most likely is making a conscious effort to be seen as an equal and to be treated with respect.

In the work environment, when both you and the person with whom you are speaking are leaning into one another as you speak or stand, it is a very good sign. It means you are in sync and the odds are in your favor that a positive business interaction will result.

If one person is leaning in and the other one is not, it means that there is conflict and disharmony among the parties. If both people lean back, it is unlikely that they will reach a successful business outcome because of the dislike, lack of trust, or differences between the parties.

There is nothing more powerful in a business interaction than when two people lean into each other to show agreement, and they subconsciously mirror each other's movements and body language. It means they are definitely on the same page.

If there is a group of people standing, the position of their toes and feet can tell a great deal about the group dynamics. If one person's feet are pointed toward another's and the pointing of the toes is not reciprocal, it means that one person feels more favorable about the other. If none of the members in the group are pointing their toes in anyone's direction, there is usually disharmony and conflict within the group.

When You Are on Your Way Out

The office assistant to your boss is often the best barometer of what is going on with your future at the company. Because she is in close contact with the boss, who might confide in her or have her prepare the necessary paperwork for your dismissal, she usually knows ahead of others what is going on with office politics and staffing. If she was once warm and bubbly to you and suddenly turns cold, rest assured you won't be working at that company much longer, especially if she is friendly to everyone else.

There are other ways you will know to start looking for another job:

1. You are no longer in the loop and given information by others as to what is going on in the company.
2. Your workload is suddenly given to others to do.
3. People don't look at you and aren't as friendly as they used to be.
4. No one asks for your help or advice.
5. People are uncomfortable around you and stop speaking when you enter a room.

In the work arena, when your boss, colleague, or client points her toes in your direction, it can mean she is comfortable dealing with you and that she likes you, which usually translates into wanting to do business with you. If, however, someone's toes are pointing toward the door or away from you, it's a sign that person wants out of the situation.

If you are meeting with someone and notice him tapping his feet and there is no music or his toes are on the ground but his heels are not, this is not a good sign. It means that he has lost interest or is restless and ready to leave.

CHAPTER 9

HOW TO SPOT NERVES, DISCOMFORT, AND DECEPTION

IN YOUR PROFESSIONAL and personal lives, you have to know who is friend or foe and who is telling you the truth or a bunch of lies. There are a number of tells that can indicate whether people are extremely distressed or anxious, which may be the result of their lying.

Just because you see a sign of deception, however, the person may not be lying. There may be other circumstances at play, which is why it is essential to avoid generalizing and instead to look for signals of deception in the correct context.

Obviously, the more signs of deception you see, the higher the odds are that the person is not being truthful with you. For instance, let's say you ask your mate whether he was at a bar last night and, in response, he scratches his nose. That gesture might not significant on its own, but if also blushes, stammers, swallows hard, blinks a lot, and shuffles his feet, then you have a substantial evidence that he's probably hiding something from you.

If you study all the signals of deception and stress in this chapter, you will become a highly astute and accurate human lie detector.

When a person has lied, changes in the body take place because there is a conflict between what the person is doing and saying and the truth.

What Breathing and Skin Changes Mean

Our breathing patterns change depending on the circumstances, such as when we are under extreme stress or tell a lie. You might notice people filling up their lungs with the maximum amount of air and then immediately releasing their breath. The reason for this is that they are oxygenating their bodies because stress and anxiety has propelled their autonomic nervous system to work overtime. It takes enormous energy to fabricate and deceive, and every system in the body—respiratory, skin, digestive, and neuromotor—kicks into high gear in response to the increased stress.

You may also see people's cheeks suddenly puff out as they release air. This action, too, is their body's attempt to release the tension it has accumulated during the stress of their deception.

When people become extremely anxious, they experience other changes, which might include their skin changing color and consistency.

For instance, in fair-skinned people, the color can change from a light shade of pink to bright red to white and even take on a grayish pallor. As their blood-flow changes, their skin reflects that change. You can easily see the color change in those with light skin, but it is much harder to observe in darker-skinned individuals, whose skin color can darken more or become ashen (grayish).

In addition to noticing color changes in the skin, you might see perspiration. When you observe someone being deceptive, you may see little beads of perspiration break out above the person's upper lip and then on her forehead, making it appear shiny. As the perspiration flows, you'll see her wipe the sweat off her forehead and brow, yet another signal of deception.

The perspiration will often migrate to the palms of the hands, making them clammy if you shake their hand or touch their palm. You'll then see them wipe their sweaty hands together or on their clothing.

Shaking is also the body's response to fear. In the liar's case, it results from the fear of getting caught.

Because the body temperature of people who are under stress or lying rises, they'll do what they can to relieve themselves of the discomfort of feeling hot, such as loosening their tie or putting their finger under their collar to loosen it. Because of the temperature change, it is also not uncommon to see the skin break out in red patches or bumps. The stress and anxiety may make them swallow hard because they feel as though their throat muscles are tightening. These are automatic reactions that seem like life-saving movements to them but that translate into warning signs of deception for you.

When blood flow changes, the veins and capillaries expand. People feel discomfort in the miniscule capillaries located throughout their body, including the delicate mucous membranes in the nose. This is why, to relieve their discomfort, people will automatically begin to pull on or scratch their nose, eye, ear, or cheek and around their mouth. Because of this itchy or uncomfortable feeling, you may see their lips swing to the side, purse together, or stretch, which is a typical indicator of deception if it occurs during questioning.

Muscle Shakes

When there is considerable muscle tension, it is not uncommon for the muscles to twitch and become weaker. As a result, the person experiences unsteadiness or shakiness. You can often see it in their hands as they lift something like a cup of water. You can see it in their legs as their gait becomes unsteady.

Shaking is also the body's response to fear. In the liar's case, it results from the fear of getting caught. The body undergoes a temperature change when it knows something frightening or uncomfortable is about to take place. So it may create a shaking or vibratory motion to help regulate the temperature change because of fear.

Most commonly, someone battling nervous tension is betrayed by the shakiness in his or her voice. The vocal muscles, which are the size of a thumbnail, become tense, sparking vocal tremors and pitch breaks when the person speaks.

What the Eyes Can Tell Us

When people blink a lot, it is a defensive reaction. For instance, if someone suddenly raised a fist and came at you, you would immediately back up and start blinking. That reaction is nature's way of clearing your eyes for better vision so you are prepared for what that other person might do to you.

When you are stressed, the same thing happens. You blink a lot as a means of defending yourself against someone who is questioning you about your misdeeds. This action can also reflect feelings of uncertainty or insecurity.

When people are embarrassed, ashamed, or uncomfortable, they will immediately look away from you. For some, it is difficult to maintain any eye contact, which is why, when you ask someone a question and she lies in response, she will shift her line of vision.

HOW PEOPLE DISPLAY SELF-SOOTHING BEHAVIORS

Feeling stress makes people uncomfortable, and they seek immediate relief from these feelings and will automatically do things that create pleasant sensations. For instance, they may rub one or both of their eyes, much like babies do when they are overtired or upset. They may repeatedly stroke certain parts of their body, like their forearm or thigh. They may scratch their head, not because it itches, but because it feels good.

The body temperature initially rises during stress and then goes into what is known as homeostatic balance and begins to cool down. The stressed-out or lying person may begin to feel a surge of coolness in his body and begin to repeatedly rub his fingers or the palms of his hands together to create warmth.

In the same way that people engage in self-soothing behaviors, they may also attempt to hurt or even mutilate themselves in an attempt to redirect the pain of their anxiety, which can make them feel better. There are also those who self-mutilate to feel worse as a means of punishing themselves. You may have seen people picking at their hands and fingers until they bleed. More commonly, you see them pinch or pull at their skin, pull their ears, bite their lips, bite their fingers or nails, scratch themselves vigorously, or even bang their heads. It is not unusual to see criminals who have been left alone in an interrogation room bang their heads against the wall or table.

Some people will continually maintain eye contact with you in an attempt to make you think they are telling the truth.

It doesn't matter whether people shift their eyes to the left or right or up or down. The main thing is that their eyes have shifted. There is a school of thought and a myth perpetuated in other books on body language that looking up means people are visually-oriented and need to be spoken to in visual terms, such as "I see" or "Look at this," while looking to the right or left means they are auditory people who can relate to terms such as "I hear you" or "Listen to this." There is no scientific evidence to support this theory, so rather than paying attention to where people look, focus on whether they break eye contact on a crucial question or when relaying significant information, which may indicate deception.

When someone suddenly squints his eyes and a furrowed line appears in the middle of his forehead during questioning, these are usually huge tells of deception. Their eye expression indicates that they are upset, annoyed, or angry that you are asking probing questions. You may also see their forehead wrinkle as they open their eyes wide, indicating both surprise at your questioning recognition of their lie.

Some people will continually maintain eye contact with you in an attempt to make you think they are telling the truth. But you should conclude just the opposite. This is a huge tell because no one who is telling the truth constantly stares at you, unless he or she is blind.

Lip and Mouth Tells

The main tell when people lie or are under extreme stress is that they have difficulty lubricating the inside of their mouth. Their mucous membranes dry out, and they subsequently have difficulty swallowing and forming words. Their tongue becomes dry and, along with their teeth, begins to stick to the inside of their upper lip. That is why you see liars or stressed-out individuals constantly lick their lips and swallow, purse their lips, and even swing their lips in a subconscious attempt to produce more saliva to relieve their discomfort.

Without enough saliva in their mouth, liars become thirsty, and it is not uncommon for them to down an entire bottle of water in one sitting. This is typically seen when a guilty person is being interrogated during a criminal investigation.

Muscle Twitching and Involuntary Muscle Action

The most common muscle twitches appear at the temples and jaw line, especially when the jaws clench together. This, too, is the autonomic nervous system at work when someone is under stress. When you see someone's temples pulsating, it is often the result of the increased blood flow and muscle tension. When the jaws clench together, that is also the result of muscular tension.

Muscle tension is also prevalent in the neck, especially at the back. Thus, it is not uncommon to see people rub the back of their neck or place their hand there when engaging in deception. Another major tell when a person lies is the shoulder shrug. It is the body's way of releasing muscular tension that occurs when a person is concocting a lie or when they are being questioned about a non-truth.

Liars may suddenly move or shuffle their feet when asked a critical question or manufacturing a lie. It is their body's way of saying they want to flee or leave the scene to get away from the questioning.

Deceptive Talk

There are many tells in a person's speech when that person is not being truthful. Here are some of the things they will do:

- Answer a question with a question
- Give a roundabout answer or go off on a tangent rather than getting to the point when responding to a question

ABDOMINAL DISTRESS AS A TELL

It is not uncommon to see highly anxious or deceptive individuals clutch their stomach or abdominal area in sudden pain or discomfort. This reaction is the autonomic nervous system going into overdrive as the digestive juices flow more rapidly and the physical digestive mechanism works harder and becomes more stressed. The abdominal pain and discomfort is the result of the peristaltic action of the intestines and the functioning of the bladder. That explains why the deceiver or an individual under extreme stress may have an urgency to defecate or urinate, feel nauseous, and even vomit as they literally purge themselves of their lies and anxiety.

- Repeat words and phrases
- Make Freudian slips in which they may admit guilt and then immediately self-correct
- Speak loudly to feign confidence, especially when questioned or confronted
- Vocally die off at the end of key phrases or sentences
- Talk too much and give too much information that isn't relevant
- Hesitate and stammer over key issues, saying "uh" and "um" a lot
- Pause for a lengthy period of time, during which they are concocting their lie
- Go on the defensive and turn the tables
- Speak in a shaky voice
- Frequently clear their throat

You may find these people in your personal life, your business dealings, and even in your family. They can be male or female, young or old. To give you the Body Language Advantage over these toxic types so you can easily recognize them and deal with them accordingly—by establishing boundaries or not allowing them into your life—I have put together a profile of each based on speech and voice patterns, body language, and facial language.

HIDING AND MASKING

As deceivers hide their words and the truth, they subconsciously make an attempt to hide physically as well. That is why you will see them hide their hands in their pockets, ball them up, hide them under the table, or even pull the sleeve of their sweater over them.

They will hide their face by covering their mouth with their hands. They will hide their eyes by looking away, or they avoid eye contact by bowing their head.

They also hide their bodies by placing their arms over their torso. And they often hide their feet as they shuffle them. If they are sitting down or standing, it is not uncommon to see them stepping on their feet in an attempt to hide them. If they are seated, they might move their feet under the chair to hide them.

CHAPTER 10

PROFILING THE TOP TEN TOXIC TYPES OF PEOPLE

THERE ARE PEOPLE WHO are toxic to us, who make our lives miserable. I have included profiles of the ten most common toxic types. They are:

1. Jealous Competitors
2. Sneaky Erupting Volcanoes
3. Know-It-Alls
4. Cheating Liars
5. Controlling Bullies
6. Backstabbing Manipulators
7. Self-Destructive Victims
8. Spineless Wimps
9. Selfish Narcissists
10. Emotionless People

1. Jealous Competitors

Speech Pattern

They compete by interrupting, contradicting, constantly disagreeing, or trying to "top" you with how much better they are or how much more they know. Often verbally abusive, there is nothing more uncomfortable than listening to a contentious competitor. They don't care who else is around because their aim is to belittle you to make them right and you wrong. Whether in a professional or social setting, they take issue with practically everything you say, no matter how benign or insignificant. Their objective is to verbally minimize you. It is not uncommon for them to use personal attacks—intimate information you shared with them in the past—as ammunition against you. Deep down they feel intimidated by you, which is at the root of their actions.

If challenged, Jealous Competitors will take the opposite point of view of the situation and find something critical or hostile to add, such as, "You don't know what you're talking about."

Voice Pattern

Rapid speech is characteristic of Jealous Competitors. They rarely allow you to get a word in edgewise. You will notice vocal tension as they try to interject what they want to say. You may also hear sarcasm, disgust, and anger in their tones as they speak.

Body Language

Their torso may lunge forward in an aggressive stance as they wait for your next move. Their rigid body posture indicates tension and conflict, and they may invade your space as a means of intimidating you or pushing your buttons. When they touch you, it isn't usually gentle, soft, and loving. Instead, it is hard, strong, and firm. They frequently touch others when speaking as a way of asserting their dominance. The way they touch may also be saying, "I don't like you and I want to hurt you."

On an intimate level, this personality type may bring a lot of passion to the early stages of a relationship, but it wears thin over time, especially when having sex becomes a competition. Their underlying agitation and tension, often displayed in fidgeting and physical uneasiness, will eventually surface. Competitive relationships can become emotionally and physically dangerous.

Facial Language

Because they feel uncomfortable and tense, it's not uncommon to see the Jealous Competitor's eyes dart around. Perhaps they are subconsciously looking for an advantage. As a result, it is difficult for them to maintain eye contact, which is essential for creating true intimacy.

Gulping or lip-licking is frequently seen when they perceive they may have lost their winning edge, no matter how insignificant. If you outshine them—by "winning" a new job, earning a raise, or proving you are right about something—you will see a serious expression come over their face, one that is devoid of emotion and belies their words if they say, "I am happy for you" or "That's great." The truth is they are not happy, nor do they feel great about your win.

2. Sneaky Erupting Volcanoes

Speech Pattern

Like Jealous Competitors, Sneaky Erupting Volcanoes may use nice words to speak to you and tell you how happy they are for you when things go your way. But the truth is that they aren't happy for you at all.

They confuse you because they make you think they're on your side and completely supportive of you. But out of the blue, they can turn on you with unexpected criticism. Sarcasm is a favorite tool with this type of toxic terror. When you're least expecting it, they'll throw something at you that you shared in confidence, followed by a sarcastic laugh and "I was only kidding."

Or they may make fun of something serious you once shared. One moment they may fawn over you, and the next, they take a verbal snipe at you. One moment you can do no wrong, and the next you are an idiot in their eyes. It becomes hard to trust them completely: How can you feel sure-footed when you don't know whether you are with a friend or foe?

Certain Sneaky Erupting Volcanoes hold in whatever upsets them and will refuse to tell you what's bothering them. Instead, they'll keep a mental score card and remember every infraction you committed over the years. Then when their mental score card is full, they will unleash a frightening torrent of vitriol. You may think they are going off on you for something insignificant, but they have stored up their anger for years, which comes out as you listen to the chronology of your "misbehaviors."

Sneaky Erupting Volcanoes rarely give you a straight and honest answer when you confront them about their emotions. They may turn silent or sulk. If you sense something is bothering them and ask what's wrong, they'll never admit anything and will say instead, "Nothing" or "I'm fine." In reality, they are angry, and they won't let you know until they are ready. On occasion, they may start to let you know, only to interrupt themselves in mid-sentence and say, "Forget it." Whether you are in a personal or business relationship, this tactic is used to sabotage you.

You may think Sneaky Erupting Volcanoes are going off on you for something insignificant, but they have stored up their anger for years . . .

Voice Pattern

Because Sneaky Erupting Volcanoes withhold their true thoughts and feelings, rarely giving you a straight and honest answer, they are secretive and tend not to reveal much about themselves. Their outward aim is to keep things on an even keel and avoid conflict. So they tend to come across as benign, easygoing, and on the quiet side, but theirs is a false façade.

When they speak, the volume of their voice often trails or dies off at the end of sentences, making it difficult to hear everything they said. This habit, along with their using softer, quieter tones, forces you to ask them to speak up. This is exactly what they want. It increases their sense of power and control to get you to pay attention, which in turn makes them feel important.

If they use a high-pitched, overly bouncy and sweet tone, it usually means they are overcompensating for negative feelings they harbor toward you.

Another way this type hides anger and jealousy is by not opening their jaws wide enough when they speak, which makes them sound nasal and lock-jawed. They may hide their anger by using a monotone that doesn't give you a true read of their emotions. Finally, if they inadvertently reveal any of their true emotions, they may laugh or cough as a sign of discomfort.

Body Language

To compensate for their negative feelings toward you, Sneaky Erupting Volcanoes may engage in nonverbal fawning by touching you a lot. In addition, you may see them rock back and forth, which is their subconscious attempt to get away from you.

Other indications that they really don't want to be in your presence is when you see them tap their feet, drum their fingers, or make other hand and foot movements that suggest they are anxious to leave. You might also notice their toes pointed in the opposite direction when they're speaking to you, which says, "I want to get out of here." Or you'll see that their hands are curled in a fist with the thumbs hidden inside the palms. This gesture shows hostile feelings.

Similarly, you'll see them cross and lock their ankles, a gesture that often reflects their attempt to hold back their true emotions. They may also jerk their head back when speaking to you or rub their neck, which indicates that they are repressing their feelings.

They will often demonstrate ambivalent feelings toward you by quickly learning toward you, which is a signal they are interested in what you have to say, and then leaning backward to indicate they are not interested in what you have to say and putting distance between you.

If they are in a personal relationship with you, they will act out these ambivalent feelings by not hugging you face to face but rather twisting their body at an angle so they are almost hugging you from the side. It's their way of physically cutting you off and maintaining distance.

Facial Language

Sneaky Erupting Volcanoes tend to have tight, pursed-lip grins, and their lips do not turn up at the corners as happens with a genuine or sincere smile. You may, however, see an uneven smile or a smirk, which is a sign of their ambivalence. They may also cup their hand over their mouth when speaking to you, which indicates they don't want to reveal how they truly feel about you. In doing this, or by biting their lower lip, they are holding back. These behaviors reflect the passive-aggressor's subconscious attempt to control angry or jealous feelings, which also explains why they find it difficult to look at you for any length of time and are constantly breaking eye contact with you.

3. Know-It-Alls

Speech Pattern

Know-It-Alls verbally degrade you and patronize you to make themselves feel better than you. Their put-downs can be subtle as they are quick-tongued and seem to have an answer for everything. There's a mechanical and rigid precision to their speech pattern as they attempt to take over conversations.

They are fundamentally close-minded, intellectual bullies who view their ideas and opinions as the only ones that matter. No one can change their opinions or open their mind to new points of view. They regularly gossip about and criticize others because they thrive on making themselves right and everyone else wrong.

They typically speak in a slow, condescending manner, showing off their knowledge as they talk at you, not with you; they speak deliberately, articulating and enunciating carefully. They'll often pepper their speech with trendy expressions, large vocabulary words, or ethnic terms as a means of showing off and letting you know how much they know.

Because they're extremely insecure, their biggest fear is not having an audience over which to feel superior. Because they are self-righteous and think they know everything, like the Selfish Narcissist, they use "I" a lot. They are self-absorbed to the point of having little regard for others' time when they are pontificating. They can take forever to tell a story or express an idea, and they will ignore you if you try to interject an opinion or ask a question. They'll often speak over you as though you aren't even there.

Because it is easy for them to depersonalize and objectify you, they are able to speak to you in a degrading manner by assaulting you with words that are spoken so violently you may feel like there are verbal bullets piercing right through you. They think nothing of openly laughing at you, teasing you, making cutting remarks or snide comments, or using sarcasm toward you, especially if they assume you don't understand what they are saying or you disagree. If you manage to get a word in edgewise and complain about their condescending treatment, they'll belittle you and sarcastically assure you that "you're misinterpreting things."

Voice Pattern

A staccato and deliberately choppy tone that lacks vocal animation is prevalent in this toxic type. This gives the Know-It-All the tonal quality of someone who is highly critical. Their hard, glottal, attacking tones reflect impatience with those whom they see as being inferior. They often sound like they are speaking to a naughty child, so it is not uncommon for them to use quieter calm tones, which forces you to listen and pay close attention to what they have to say, similar to other toxic types.

Body Language

If you confront them or respond to their droning, condescending pontification, you'll see them become impatient and start to fidget and move around. More than anything, though, you'll see a stiff, erect stance as they lean backward to maintain an air of distance from others. They are frequently seen with their hands placed on their hips, elbows extended. This is a body language signal that others should keep their distance.

Know-It-Alls will expose the back of their hand, which indicates they may be closed off to others and that reciprocal communication and interaction isn't welcome. They may also use a pincer grip with their thumb touching their index finger when speaking to emphasize the precision of what they are attempting to say. When bored or annoyed with you, it is not unusual to see them interlock their fingers and twiddle their thumbs. You might also see them steeple their fingertips together and raise them in front of their chest and under their chin while conveying their opinions in a know-it-all attitude. This body language is usually accompanied by a backward tilt of the head, giving them a snob-like air.

They may point at you when speaking to further display a sense of superiority over you. If you get too close and invade their space, or if they want to emphasize a point, don't be surprised to see them aggressively pointing a finger in front of you.

Facial Language

It's not uncommon to see Know-It-Alls with a condescending smirk or a phony, forced, tight-lipped grin. This false smile is an expression of their disrespect as they look down at you. In fact, you may see them lift their chin and literally look down their nose at you when speaking.

You may see them partially close their eyes, raise their eyebrows, and purse their lips in an attempt to cut you off and down. Not looking directly at you allows them to further objectify you and continue their condescending, abusive way of communicating.

If you confront them, don't be surprised if you see them roll their eyes, indicating disgust and annoyance that you would dare question or talk back to them. This is often accompanied by a backward jerk of their head, which means they have literally been taken aback. You may notice their eyes darting around the room, seeking out people more interesting and important than you. In a restaurant, they may speak to people at neighboring tables while ignoring you.

4. Cheating Liars

Speech Pattern

This toxic type can fool a number of people for a long time. Cheating Liars tend to be extremely complimentary toward you. Even if you don't initially believe what they say, they are so convincing that you eventually start believing them. They constantly feed your ego, so you want to be around them. They are usually overly friendly when they first meet you, behavior that is typical of con men and women.

The flip side of their feel-good banter is they can direct it toward others at a moment's notice. Just as great as they make you feel through their words, they do the same to others who fall into their seductive clutches.

One way that Cheating Liars are able to turn the tables on you is through the vocal tones they use to manipulate you, which are usually low, gentle, slow, and seductive.

If you accuse them of flirting or cheating, don't be surprised when they turn the tables on you and try to make you think you're the one with the problem or that you must have imagined what you think you saw. With their amazing ability to twist your words, they know exactly what to say to turn the conversation to their favor.

More dangerous liars, for example, con men and women or sociopaths, have a distinct voice quality and speech characteristics that are described below. With cheating con men and women, they tend never to miss a beat when you catch them in a lie. They engage in circumlocution ("beating around the bush") or they turn the course of the conversation as though nothing had happened. They remain unflappable even after they have been busted. They will simply and casually change the subject.

Voice Pattern

One way that Cheating Liars are able to turn the tables on you is through the vocal tones they use to manipulate you, which are usually low, gentle, slow, and seductive. They know how to create a sensuous breathiness when speaking. Because they often harbor a great deal of vocal tension as a result of distorting or hiding the truth, their throat muscles can easily tighten up. Because of the discomfort in their throat, you will regularly hear them clearing their throat as they engage in lies.

Additionally, you will hear breaks in the pitch of their voice as their vocal muscles tense up in the midst of their lies. The pitch of their voice may also go up, which is the result of the muscle tension in their vocal cords.

Cheating Liars tend engage in a lot of fast, energetic talking, especially when they are about to initiate a con.

Body Language

Cheating Liars shrug their shoulders, shuffle their feet, rotate their feet inward for a pigeon-toed posture, tilt their head to the side, hide their hands as they speak, fidget, and rock back and forth to express their uneasiness—or do the opposite by sitting or standing perfectly still and appearing rigid. When sitting, they also tend to place their hands on their lap without moving them.

When they first meet you, they usually invade your space right away, getting physically close to let you know they like you and are interested in what you do and say. They may "accidentally" brush up against you and let their touch linger to further demonstrate their interest. Because most Cheating Liars feel comfortable in their own bodies, there is no doubt that their relaxed stance makes others feel comfortable around them.

Whether male or female, they may assume a sexual posture by rolling their shoulders back and exposing their torso to elicit more attention from the opposite sex. To further attract attention, Cheating Liars may play with their hair, put their fingers on their lips, rub their hands or arms, and hug or hold on to themselves for no apparent reason. These forms of self-stimulation give them a sense of physical comfort.

If you ask them a direct question, such as, "Were you with Bob last night?" they'll often rub, knead, or scratch any part of their body. In doing so, they comfort themselves and give themselves physical relief. The more unnerved and uncomfortable they feel, the more you'll see these gestures. Finally, they may speak to you with their palms up, giving the impression that they are begging you to believe them as they try to explain away their lie.

Facial Language

When Cheating Liars want to reel in their prey, they never want to lose eye contact, and they know how to hold a gaze beyond the normal two to three seconds. They tilt their head in the direction of their victim, nod with approval whenever the other person speaks—whether or not they agree—and mirror that person's facial expressions.

They also tend to exhibit a number of other seductive facial movements, including smiling in a relaxed way, showing their upper teeth, combining a sexy lip pout with a fixed gaze, and lightly licking their lips. You will notice their non-blinking, lying eyes and tight-lipped, phony smile. They'll blink excessively when confronted and often place their fingers over their lips while they speak.

5. Controlling Bullies

Speech Pattern

Controlling Bullies are verbally belligerent, constantly spewing hostile words and phrases, and always ready for verbal warfare. Because their mantra is "my way or the highway," challenging them will usually be met with a tirade of screaming, shouting, and interrupting.

They think nothing of abusing you with a barrage of degrading curse words. They use controlling phrases such as, "I'm going to let you," "I'll allow you," or "I'll give you my permission to." They also tell you what they won't allow you to do by saying: "I don't want you to," "I forbid you to," or "You can't." They are basically speaking to you as if you were a disobedient child.

Some Controlling Bullies will allow you to do what you want to do as long as it conforms to their rules. For example, they may say, "You can visit your mother, but only if you are back before dinner." They are highly critical of what you look like, how you dress, where you go, what you do, what you eat, and how much money you spend, even if you are the breadwinner. They'll try to control all of your basic freedoms, often threatening you if you try to assert yourself, by making warning statements such as, "You don't want to see me angry." You should take these threats seriously because they usually mean what they say.

Voice Pattern

There is an alarmist vocal quality with this toxic type, as though there is always impending danger. And there is! Controlling Bullies often possess such hostility toward themselves and others that it can't help but come out in their voice. They try to intimidate you through a rapid-fire, clipped, booming voice, making hard, glottal attacks when speaking, and communicating in contemptuous tones.

When you don't obey them or they feel like they are losing control, their tones get louder as they get angrier, and they don't care who hears them yell. Their main concern is for you to obey and not challenge them. You'll rarely hear an upward inflection that would indicate a request; instead, you'll only hear harsh, loud, demanding barks as they take sadistic pleasure in making you squirm.

Body Language

Their body language reflects the same harshness and anger you hear in their voice and speech patterns. Controlling Bullies have an aggressive body stance, and they appear to lunge forward when sitting, standing, or walking. They may also invade your personal space as a way of intimidating you.

Their handshake and touches aren't gentle, but rather firm, hard, or even hurtful. They use a lot of arm movement, frequently point their finger at you, or, if you are in an intimate relationship, grab you physically when making a point. Because they tend to be angry at you and the world, they will close their fists to forcefully emphasize what they're saying to you.

Facial Language

Their tense facial expression typically includes a furrowed brow, a narrow gaze in which they almost close their eyes as they peer at you, a hard stare, and flared nostrils. Their lips are usually pursed tightly, even when they're listening. When they speak, they tend to do so with a closed jaw, indicating inner anger and hostility. As another sign of aggression, they tend to thrust their lower jaw forward.

If they are very angry, you'll see rapid eye blinking, forceful breathing through flared nostrils, a flushed face, and eyes opened wide, showing you the whites of their eyes all around the iris. If you see these facial signals, get out of their way because they may cause you great harm.

6. Backstabbing Manipulators

Speech Pattern

Backstabbing Manipulators are quick to give you their unsolicited opinions on how to run your life. Highly opinionated and undiplomatic, they speak in critical, bold, and blunt terms. Common words and phrases include: "You should," "Why don't you," "Don't do" or "Do," "You must," and "You better." They have the keen ability to twist your words and turn what you say against you by using confusion tactics. Often accusatory, they'll insist you said something you never said, mean something you never meant, or felt something you never felt as they exaggerate or misinterpret your words and actions. You can't defend yourself, set the record straight, or explain what you meant because they will insist you said something and tell you what you meant.

They also can be charming if they want, which adds to their credibility when trying to turn others against you or turn you against others. They'll think nothing of betraying someone's confidences, including yours. They'll throw secrets you have shared with them back at you, just to rile you or make you feel insecure. In fact, they thrive on this type of toxic behavior.

They are also huge gossips—as a means of amusing themselves and gaining power over you. Their conversation consists mostly of saying negative things about others to you and vice versa. Rest assured that if they are constantly trashing others to you, they are trashing you to others.

They are also the master of the sarcastic quip and the backhanded compliment. They'll say negative things about people to goad you into reacting so they can create drama and trouble.

Voice Pattern

Backstabbing Manipulators speak rapidly and in an alarmist fashion, as though there is an urgency to do something or impending danger. That's how they get you to do what they want—by confusing you and inciting your emotions so you spring into action.

They may speak loudly, with a lot of dramatic animation, to generate excitement and hold your interest. They may also use hushed and breathy tones when gossiping or giving you "privileged" information—a secret for your ears only. They use these quiet tones as a means of control and manipulation.

Body Language

They tend to invade your space, especially when giving you "privileged information."

Being physically animated—pacing and using a lot of arm and hand motion—keeps you focused on them. The more they want to alarm you, the more animated they become. You will see this when they insist you take immediate action, turn your words around, or try to convince you that you said something you never said. When speaking, their head and body move around a great deal.

They use a lot of finger-pointing when they tell you what you should and shouldn't do. It's not uncommon to see them grip their thumb and fingertips together when they're trying to make a point. They give you the impression that they are literally holding on to each and every word as they dole out just what they want you to hear and know.

Facial Language

Their tendency to speak negatively is usually reflected in their facial expression. That's why you'll often see a furrowed brow and tight lips. When they are trying to incite you, you'll see a look of alarm on their face, with wide-open eyes and mouth. Because they know they're provoking and manipulating or telling you things that may not be true, you may see considerable eye blinking or lip licking.

Because Self-Destructive Victims see themselves as sacrificial lambs, they consistently mention how much they have had to suffer and how they don't feel worthy of good things and always expect bad things to happen.

7. Self-Destructive Victims

Speech Pattern

Self-Destructive Victims are in tremendous emotional pain, which is why they sound so negative and feel so worthless. They want to destroy themselves and, unfortunately, they intend to take you with them.

Because they often hide their true feelings and inner pain, they will lash out by blaming themselves and others. When they lash out at themselves, you'll usually hear them make self-disparaging remarks, such as how stupid they are or how "it's just their luck" that everything bad happens to them. As they constantly complain and try to explain why things are so bad, they frequently refer to their past, which gives them an even bleaker view of their present and future.

They are master excuse makers for why things never work out for them or why they, in their current position, have difficulty taking responsibility for their actions. Any positive suggestion is met with a negative "yeah, but" for why things won't work.

Because Self-Destructive Victims see themselves as sacrificial lambs, they consistently mention how much they have had to suffer and how they don't feel worthy of good things and always expect bad things to happen. If you say something positive or encouraging, it will usually be met with a negative, self-abusive comment. They'll either ignore your compliment or words of encouragement or tell you why you are wrong and how you don't know what you are talking about.

In addition to blaming themselves, they are quick to blame everyone and everything for their hopeless situation. It is other people's fault they are doing self-destructive things.

Because they don't have much self-esteem and they feel their social and business relationships won't work out anyway, you'll often hear them say things that will purposely create hurtful feelings or provoke an argument at home and work. This is especially true when things are going well in their professional and personal relationships. They will immediately say something to mess it up and alienate others. Then they will admit it was their fault and tell you how they can never do anything right as a ploy to gain sympathy.

However, they'll keep saying the same toxic things to cause disharmony at work and home because they don't feel they deserve to be happy. They have a subconscious desire to destroy their most meaningful and important relationships.

If they are self-destructing with drugs or alcohol, be prepared for a barrage of rage and violence hurled at you in the form of cursing and unfounded, hateful accusations. Sadly, these verbal attacks are reflections of their self-hatred and inner agony.

Voice Pattern

Their voice usually sounds depressed, with a low-pitched monotone that is devoid of animation. In addition, the timbre of their voice may sound weak from time to time, depending on how victimized they feel at a particular moment. These vocal characteristics clearly reflect inner sadness and feelings of powerlessness.

Their voice is especially soft when describing how poorly they've been mistreated by others. When complaining or explaining, it's not uncommon to hear a nasal whine, especially as their pitch goes up at the end of statements, making them sound vulnerable and victim-like. Without even listening to their words, the tone alone says, "Can you believe this is happening to poor me?"

Yelling and verbal abuse are not uncommon, especially if they are blaming you or someone else for their predicament. This is particularly evident if they have been drinking, doing drugs, or engaging in other self-destructive behaviors. You may also hear tonal swings that quickly shift from self-pitying whimpers to loud, jolting, and hateful thunderous tones.

Body Language

Self-Destructive Victims often have poor posture with slouching shoulders, as though they are carrying the entire weight of the world. In assuming this posture, they tend to minimize themselves. You might also see them with arms folded across their chest as a subconscious means of self-protection. Their head is often bowed so they appear to be looking up when talking to others.

If you try to comfort or challenge them with suggestions for getting out of their victim state, they may respond with a restless, rocking back-and-forth motion. In addition, they often fidget, pick or bite their nails or fingers, or wring their hands.

Shuffling their feet or crossing and uncrossing their legs is also typical. To comfort themselves into feeling more secure, they may clasp their hands together or hold on to their arms or legs when listening or speaking.

They frequently take out their bad feelings on themselves by drinking, overeating, or using drugs, and they also take them out on other people or things. That's why it's not uncommon to see them drive recklessly, punch holes in walls, or even resort to physical violence toward others.

Facial Language

Their eyes tend to narrow when speaking because of muscle tension around their eyelids, brows, and forehead. Their lips are often tense, especially around the corners, indicating repressed anger and chronic sadness. When they feel uneasy and anxious, they frequently bite their lower lip. There is a consistent facial mask of tension and sadness. They will usually look down, maintain poor eye contact, and rotate their eyes downward to reflect shame. If they have been verbally abusive, they usually won't look at you because they feel ashamed of their out-of-control behavior.

8. Spineless Wimps

Speech Pattern

Spineless Wimps can't confront anyone so they stray from any communication they perceive as challenging or uncomfortable. Because they can't face direct communication, they usually avoid it by being silent, engage in circumlocution, or refuse to give you a straight answer.

They tend to be people of few words who choose their words carefully so as not to offend anyone. Because they are reluctant to commit to a single point of view, they tend to couch everything they say in preambles and present multiple points of view. These types are essentially "sheeple" (sheep + people) who follow the herd and do what everyone else does because they don't have a mind of their own.

In an attempt not to make waves or offend, they become what they fear most: They become offensive by being evasive.

Voice Pattern

Spineless Wimps speak softly, and their sentences tend to die off at the end, making it difficult to hear them. Because they don't want to make a mistake or say the wrong thing, they will speak slowly, measuring each word. There may be long pauses between words and phrases as they carefully think about what they will say before saying it. You can hear fear in their voice, which is characterized by tentative, hesitant tones, and they frequently repeat words and phrases. This vocal pattern reveals that they aren't being totally honest or forthright with you. In attempting not to offend you, they won't tell you the truth about what they are really thinking. Throat clearing is another giveaway that they are not being completely candid. You may also hear shakiness in the voice, especially when they are confronted or pressed to make a choice.

Body Language

You will see a lot of head scratching when they are asked a question they don't want to answer, indicating confusion and discomfort. And they usually have a weak or limp touch because they are afraid to make the first move.

Another display of insecurity and timidity is in their posture, which is often slouched, with shoulders positioned forward. They may rock back and forth when they feel uncomfortable.

It is not uncommon to see their toes turned inward, as if they're pigeon-toed, which is a sign of resignation or submission. Arms folded across their chest or body, as a means of subconsciously protecting themselves from emotional discomfort, may also be evident. They may hold on to themselves or an object in order to "brace" themselves when confronted. A bowed head is another strategy for avoiding communication, and it reflects their submission.

Facial Language

When feeling intimidated, which is most of the time, Spineless Wimps will go to great lengths to avoid eye or face contact. They will look to the right, left, up, or down, anywhere but directly at you. If confronted or forced to make a decision, they will typically look down at their feet. There is often an expression of fear and tension on their face, reflected in their eyebrows being drawn

Selfish Narcissists don't really care about what you have to say or anything you contribute to the conversation. Instead, they will keep talking until they are done.

together and forehead being furrowed. Lip biting and a retracted chin often indicate their lack of confidence and uneasiness. You may also see signs of their anxiety when they blush or blotches appear on their neck.

9. Selfish Narcissists

Speech Pattern

Selfish Narcissists have an insatiable need to talk about themselves and receive praise. If these needs aren't met, you'll hear them fishing for compliments. They often make self-aggrandizing comments and ask you to agree with them, such as, "I'm brilliant, wouldn't you agree?" Or they will tell you what great things others have said about them, both to reassure themselves and to let you know that others find them wonderful, beautiful, or sexy.

The words "I", "me," "myself," and "mine" are most prevalent in their vocabulary. Whenever they use the word "you," it is usually in the context of what you can do for them or how great you feel about them.

If the topic of conversation is not them, they become bored and lose interest. It's difficult to have a dialogue with them because they seem to redirect almost everything back to themselves.

Selfish Narcissists don't really care about what you have to say or anything you contribute to the conversation. Instead, they will keep talking until they are done. They are quick to change the subject or interrupt because they only want to talk about what interests them.

They speak with a sense of entitlement, and it is not uncommon to hear them exaggerate. Because they tend to be attracted to vulnerable types, over whom they can feel superior, they will often encourage their victim to talk about problems and will continue dealing with them only if they offer a huge amount of enthusiastic adulation and appreciation for what they are doing to help them. They are partial to those who have been traumatized because these people tend to feel needy and grateful when someone is there to help rescue them. If the traumatized victim starts to recover, stand on his or her own feet, and no longer needs their help, Selfish Narcissists are off to find their next victim—but not until they have berated the ungrateful victim for no longer adoring or praising them or needing their help. They emotionally punish anyone who lets them down or for a perceived slight.

Abusive comments such as, "If it wasn't for me, you'd be nowhere," are usually followed by telling their victims how bad they are and making derogatory and belittling comments to them. They may pull out all of their verbal ammunition to debase and humiliate the "ungrateful" victim. They usually won't let up until they have had the sadistic satisfaction of reducing the person to tears.

Voice Pattern

Because of their extreme need for attention, Selfish Narcissists will do whatever it takes to be noticed. That is why they usually speak in an obnoxious tone, whereby they speak and laugh loudly, all the while looking around to make sure people notice them.

Because Selfish Narcissists like to show off and need an audience, they tend to engage people by using a highly animated, over-the-top voice pattern, especially when in public. Their switch is almost always "on" as they try to impress you.

If they are not the center of attention, you'll hear monotonous, short-clipped tones that indicate boredom. They may even yawn and sigh if they feel forced to listen to what they consider to be your verbal drivel. If they feel slighted or you aren't giving them enough attention, they may start to raise their voice like a child, so everyone hears them and turns in their direction.

Body Language

Because they are so enamored with themselves, they give off an air of confidence that is conveyed through their body with a straight, upright posture. Their head is usually tilted upward, which keeps their eyes in the proper alignment to see who's looking at and noticing them.

When they speak to people about their one and only topic—themselves—you will see them leaning in to others. As soon as the topic veers away from them, you can visibly see them backing off and leaning away.

Selfish Narcissists tend to invade other people's space and take up a lot of room when standing or sitting. To call attention to their presence, they will use a lot of hand and arm movements, and they think nothing of touching others to get them to focus on them. They have been known to throw tantrums, objects, and even their fists when they don't get enough attention.

Facial Language

When their needs are met and they get enough attention, they'll smile genuinely, with eyes crinkling and lips spread and relaxed. They seem to have a sparkle in their eye, and they light up when they feel acknowledged and appreciated. When not looking in the mirror, they maintain great eye and face contact with their "fans." They will look directly at them and scan their faces for expressions of approval and adulation when talking about themselves. But if their adoring fans look away or lose interest, their happy smile immediately turns into a tight-lipped frown.

If Selfish Narcissists are not the topic of conversation, a glazed look of boredom will come over them, and they will visually disconnect. If they are in a relationship where they don't receive constant attention and approval, their facial language will show anger, complete with knitted brow, furrowed forehead, and a narrowed, steely gaze.

10. Emotionless People

Speech Pattern

Emotionless People are verbally stingy. They are people of few words who speak when spoken to. They are not ones to initiate conversations. Typically methodical and task-oriented, they keep things close to the vest, rarely betraying feelings or emotions. When confronted about their lack of expression, they'll often respond with, "That's just not me. I'm not that type of person," "I'm not an emotional person," "I don't like to talk much," or "I don't talk about my feelings." Because they don't let you know how they feel, you're always second-guessing them as they leave you feeling unsettled and unsure.

If you married an emotionless person thinking you can change him or her, you are wrong. That's who they are and how they will stay. They can only change if they want to.

They will insist on showing love for you in ways that make them feel comfortable. They aren't being abusive; that's just who they are. If a man or woman is uncommunicative, withholds affection, or doesn't respond to your emotions, it is mental and emotional cruelty and nothing less than abuse.

On the other hand, there are certain disorders, such as autism or Asperger's syndrome, where this kind of uncommunicative behavior is not uncommon. Having such a disorder does not preclude someone from engaging in a meaningful, intimate relationship. There just has to be a great deal of awareness and acceptance on the part of the mate and willingness for the person with the disorder to participate in behavioral therapy to improve his or her communication skills.

Voice Pattern

Emotionless People usually speak in a monotone, which indicates detachment from you as they depersonalize you. Because they don't use vocal animation, it's impossible to decipher how they really feel. They are vocally repressed and have a tendency to be rigid and inflexible. They usually speak in clipped, mechanical tones and tend to hyper-articulate their words.

Body Language

Their body language is usually rigid with ramrod, soldier-like postures and mechanical gestures. This tends to make others uncomfortable because they feel as though the emotionless person is judging them or doesn't like them.

They make guarded movements and don't often touch others. If they do touch or hug, it is usually stiff and awkward. You may see them cover their body by crossing their arms over their chest.

Their head is usually erect, another illustration of their defensiveness, protectiveness, and rigidity. They tend to angle their body away from you when hugging or kissing you, which suggests that they're cutting you off from their affection. They may keep their hands on their lap or hold on to themselves when interacting with others to feel more secure and in control.

Facial Language

Emotionless People often have a blank or monotonous facial expression. Their jaw is usually rigid and the chin is retracted, which indicates, in a primitive sort of way, that they are on the lookout for physical or emotional threats. They have poor eye contact, if any at all.

They frequently display a tight, controlled smile. If they feel threatened or uncomfortable, you'll see tension in their facial muscles. If they happen to kiss you, their kisses are often quick, tight-lipped, and perfunctory.

THE BODY LANGUAGE ADVANTAGE CAN SAVE YOUR LIFE

JUST BY KNOWING what certain body and facial language, voice, and speech signals mean, you can gain the Body Language Advantage in both your personal and business life. The more you practice reading others, the more astute you will become and the fewer mistakes you will make in your judgments and interactions with people.

But the Body Language Advantage is not just for those two aspects of your life. It can be used to save your life during these trying and confusing times in which we live. We can no longer wear blinders and refuse to see what exists in the world. The reality is that we live in a world where danger unfortunately exists. We need to know how to recognize it at a moment's notice. Our survival and that of our loved ones can depend on it.

Body Language That Says a Thief Is in Your Presence

For instance, we need to be aware that when a stranger comes up to us and touches our arm to establish rapport or places a hand over our shoulder when they ask for directions, they may be using the other hand to reach into our back pocket and take our wallet.

Body Language That Says You Are Being Manipulated

We need to be aware of how the repeated, rhythmic cadence of a televised message may just be a ploy to get you to buy something, instead of a sincere claim that the product will change your life in thirty days. The only life it will change in thirty days is the person raking in the money from doing the commercial that has sucked you in.

We need to be able to quickly see through the gushing charm and flattering proposals of marriage when we have only known someone for a few hours or days. We need to see and hear what it is, not what we fantasize it to be. We need relationships in which there are no ulterior motives, like taking you for all that you are worth. We need to be able to detect others' motivations by how they move, speak, and most of all, by what they say. We need to be able to tell when someone's emotion is real or when it is being used to manipulate us.

We need to listen carefully for signals of manipulation and watch for signals of deception as we navigate the world. Anyone who tells you how to get rich quick is the only one who will be making millions overnight by taking your money and anyone else's that he can swindle.

Body Language That Says You May End Up a Crime Victim

You need to trust your gut when you hear a monotone voice devoid of emotion, just as you need to trust it when you hear an overly animated, pushy, manipulative-sounding voice that tries to make you feel guilty or stupid for not listening and doing what is being asked of you.

Likewise, you need to trust your gut when you are about to go into a store and see someone outside whose body language doesn't seem right to you. Perhaps they are staggering, shouting, or

You need to trust your instincts when you observe that someone is unusually quiet, extremely volatile and agitated, or sweet-talking you.

gesturing wildly. Perhaps there is a large group of young men entering the store at once and then spreading out in different directions as in a flash mob. Perhaps there are those who walk in an unusual way and keep touching and patting the front of their pants. Trusting your instincts by leaving right away may end up saving your life. Perhaps the wildly gesturing man was delusional and preparing to attack the next person who tried to enter the store. Perhaps the group of men was a gang about to create mayhem. Perhaps they walked funny because some had guns in the back of their waistbands while others were patting their abs because their weapons were stashed in the front of their pants. Although you may not have known why they were doing what they were doing, the fact that you noticed something was off about their body language may have saved your life.

You need to trust your instincts when you observe that someone is unusually quiet, extremely volatile and agitated, or sweet-talking you. If something strikes you as odd, rest assured that it is.

Body Language That Says You May Get Abused

If you are in a relationship and a heated discussion escalates to the point where the other person is dripping with sweat, clenching his jaw until you see it pulsate, and poking his finger in your chest, you need to know that the next time, instead of poking a finger at you in anger, he may become violent. Get out of the relationship as soon as you can.

Body Language That Says You Are Being Lied To

Watch out for a shoulder shrug, rapidly blinking eyes, shuffling feet, or speech that includes way too much information and goes off on tangents when you're asking about an affair or other bad behavior such as drinking or taking drugs. Recognizing these signs will prevent you from being made a sucker or the victim of lies.

Body Language That Indicates a Sexual Predator

Know that a predator tests his prey with his hands—touching a child just to see whether he or she pulls away or accepts the touch. If the child pulls away, a predator will find a child who doesn't. Teaching your children never to let anyone touch them or to pull away the instant anyone does may save their life—or may save them from the emotional and psychological trauma of sexual molestation.

Molesters give gifts and speak in soft, endearing tones, offering to help the child with any problem he or she may have. Knowing this, you must teach your children never to accept gifts from anyone and to tell their problems only to you, the family doctor, or a therapist.

Body Language That Says Someone May Take Your Money

Few people would have suspected mild-mannered Bernard Madoff, who is serving a life sentence in a federal penitentiary, of stealing billions in a Ponzi scheme. But on careful inspection, his standoffish, secretive behavior, condescending arrogance, and bullying are typical of those who ended up behind bars for ripping people off at such a staggering level. With this type, a monotone voice devoid of emotion and consistently clenched hands are other giveaways. They reflect detachment and inner tension at not being found out. Sudden bursts of hostility and anger for seemingly no reason are a way of releasing what is gnawing at them on the inside.

Therefore, if you notice your financial handlers not communicating with you openly or addressing your questions and concerns in a frank, accommodating manner, you should consider finding someone else to handle your hard-earned life savings.

Body Language That Says You Are with a Potential Abuser

When a man or woman makes an overly grand display of affection, like sending you two dozen roses after meeting you the night before, it is a bad sign. Being overly charming and making plans

Know that when a stranger approaches you, acts submissive, and wants your help, think twice, especially if the person is persistent and approaches you several times.

with you for the rest of your life by promising to take you to exotic places may seem romantic, but it can also signal danger. After they have reeled you in and you are enjoying expensive gifts from them, you will notice them wanting to change your appearance to suit them

Then, after they have taken control of your appearance, they'll move on to how often and whether you can see your friends and family as they try to isolate you from everyone you know. If you don't do what they say, they may get verbally and then physically violent, which will end with apologies and "I am sorry" gifts. When this cycle repeats itself and you have endured too many of these roller-coaster incidents and you try to break up, you may be met with more violence and even threats of suicide if you try to leave. You can avoid getting involved with this kind of abuser by looking for the body language signs of excessive charm and gift-giving.

Body Language That Tells You Your Child Is on Drugs

Too many parents are shocked to discover their child is addicted to drugs. But if they had watched their child's body language and listened to his or her voice and speech pattern, they may have been able to help their child before it was too late.

For example, they may have noted that their child's disheveled look, open sores, constant scratching, overly animated facial expressions, and rotting teeth were the result of being on methamphetamines. If they had paid closer attention to their child's rapid eye movement or jaw clenching, they would have known their child was on Ecstasy, or that the runny nose, dilated pupils, frequent lip licking, and excessive body movement was because their child was using cocaine. And if they had carefully listened to their child's slurred and monotonous speech pattern and noticed a dull or vacant facial expression, they may have known that their child was abusing heroin.

Body Language That Says You May Get Killed

Know that when a stranger approaches you, acts submissive, and wants your help, think twice, especially if the person is persistent and approaches you several times as they may want to do you harm. Never help a vulnerable stranger on your own. Enlist the help of others and never go anywhere with strangers, no matter how convincing their story or how harmless they may seem.

Don't read *The Body Language Advantage* and then put it away. Instead you should keep it close at hand and refer to it periodically to refresh your memory about what to watch for. Doing so promises to enrich your life in every way.

ABOUT THE AUTHOR

LILLIAN GLASS, Ph.D., is an internationally known, well-respected authority in the area of body language and communication. She is also a media personality, where her body language analysis of newsmakers is in demand on television, magazine, and Internet outlets.

As the body language expert to such shows as *Dancing with the Stars*, *Millionaire Matchmaker*, and *Entertainment Tonight*, Dr. Glass has not only used her talents and abilities in the entertainment industry but also in the legal field, where she serves as a jury consultant and expert witness in the area of behavioral analysis and vocal forensics.

The author of more than a dozen books, including the best-selling *Toxic People*, Dr. Glass lectures worldwide and makes her body language services and products available to the public at www.drlillianglass.com.